Taylor's Pocket Guide to

Annuals

Taylor's Pocket Guide to

Annuals

A N N R E I L L Y
Consulting Editor

A Chanticleer Press Edition

Houghton Mifflin Company

Boston

For information about
permission to reproduce selections from this book,
write to Permissions,
Houghton Mifflin Company, 2 Park Street,
Boston, Massachusetts 02108

Based on Taylor's Encyclopedia of Gardening, Fourth Edition,
Copyright © 1961 by Norman Taylor,
revised and edited by
Gordon P. DeWolf, Jr.

Prepared and produced by Chanticleer Press, New York
Typeset by Dix Type, Inc., Syracuse, New York
Printed and bound by
Dai Nippon, Tokyo, Japan

Library of Congress Catalog Card Number: 89-85031
ISBN: 0-395-52244-7

DNP   10   9   8   7   6   5   4   3   2   1

CONTENTS

GARDENING WITH
ANNUALS

No matter how complete your landscape may seem—with stately trees, flowering shrubs framing the house, and a lush green lawn—it may lack the finishing touch that flowering annuals provide. Throughout the spring, summer, and fall, annuals will enhance the beauty of your home with color.

Annual flowers bring a profusion of colors and shapes at very small cost. Both beginning gardeners and experienced horticulturists welcome the almost infinite variety that annuals provide; you can plant different annuals year after year and never run out of choices.

You can easily combine annuals with perennials, shrubs, bulbs, or ornamental vegetables; but these graceful and colorful flowers can stand alone, too. Plant an island of annual color to enliven a green expanse of lawn, or a small bed of pansies near the front door to add a cheerful touch in spring before many other annuals bloom.

What Is an Annual?

An annual can be defined as a plant that grows, flowers, sets seed, and dies in the same year. For the gardener, this growth cycle translates into instant color, for annual flowers bloom very quickly. Their bloom span, which can range from one to six months, is longer than that of most perennials.

The term "annual" is also loosely applied to certain tender perennials and biennials that cannot survive the winter outside of very mild climates, but which can be grown as if they were annuals during the summer in other areas.

Depending on their tolerance of heat or cold, flowering annuals fall into one of three classes: tender annuals, half-hardy annuals, and hardy annuals. Tender annuals are subject to damage from frost; they are planted in warm soil in spring after all danger of frost has passed. In the south, a second planting can be made in midsummer for a fall display of color. Half-hardy annuals are those that will tolerate cool weather but will not withstand heavy frost. They can be planted in spring several weeks before the anticipated date of the last frost. Hardy annuals are not killed by frost. They can be planted in spring as soon as the soil can be worked. In mild areas, they can be planted in fall for early bloom the next year.

You will also see that some annuals are classified as warm-season or cool-season plants. The warm-season plants need summer heat to grow well; the cool-season ones do best in coastal areas, at high altitudes, or in the northern part of the country. In areas where they cannot survive summer heat, cool-season annuals can be grown in spring or fall.

The planting dates for tender and half-hardy biennials and perennials grown as annuals depend on the individual plant. Some can be planted in early spring or mid-spring; others grow better in warm soil and should be planted after danger of frost has passed. The individual plant accounts tell you the proper planting time for all annuals.

Getting Started

No matter how much you like a particular combination of annuals, remember that your garden will not grow well if you do not select plants whose needs are met by your environmental conditions. Before you purchase seeds or plants, you should evaluate the light, climate, soil, and water conditions in your garden. Then you will be ready to choose your annuals.

Sun and Shade

The amount of sunlight needed for growth varies from one plant to another. Every plant account in this book tells you how much light a particular annual requires: full sun, light shade, partial shade, or full shade.

Most annuals grow better if they receive their sun in the morning hours and are protected from the drying heat of the afternoon sun. This is especially true in very hot areas. Annuals that need full sun require six hours or more of direct sunlight each day. An annual that prefers light shade may receive lightly dappled sun all day or four to six hours of direct sun. Partial shade means about four hours of direct sun, or a full day of dappled shade—such as you would find under trees. If you have less than four hours of direct sun daily, choose plants that grow in full shade.

Climate

In planning your annual garden, considerations of climate are critical. Where growing seasons are long enough, it is possible to have three annual gardens in one season—a spring garden made up of cool-weather annuals, a summer bed of warm-season annuals, and a third round of color in fall with cool-season annuals. The climate will also determine your planting dates, which will be discussed later.

Some gardens have microclimates—small pockets that, because of altitude, exposure, light, or other factors, vary from the general climate in the area. A garden enclosed by a wall, for example, will be warmer than an exposed area. The area at the bottom of a hill is usually cooler than a spot halfway up the hill. When making a list of annuals for your garden plan, be sure to take into account these factors. By working with your microclimates, you may be able to grow annuals whose requirements are different from the conditions prevailing in your area of the country.

Soil and Water

Considerations regarding soil and water go very much hand in hand: Dry areas tend to have light soil, while areas with heavy rainfall or nearby water sources often have heavy soil. Choose annuals whose soil and moisture requirements match the conditions in your area. You can expand your options somewhat by improving or amending your soil (see instructions below).

Designing an Annual Garden

Once you have decided which annuals will grow best in your garden, you need to decide on a planting scheme. The first choice to make is whether to plant your flowers in beds or in borders; the decision depends on personal preference, space, and time for maintenance. Beds are plantings that are accessible from all sides (such as a planting in the middle of the lawn); borders are accessible only from one to three sides and are usually located in front of a wall, fence, hedge, or foundation planting.

Beds can be any size or shape as long as they are in proportion to their surroundings and not so wide that you can't get to the middle. Borders deeper than five feet will be difficult to work. Place your bed or border anywhere you like, to provide an accent, hide an eyesore, line the way to the front door, or unite the landscape.

Choosing Colors

Your choice of color can reflect your personality. The warm hues—red, orange, and yellow—are exciting and draw attention to a spot, while the cool colors—blue and purple—are more soothing and quieter.

If you're a novice at color design, choose one main color and one or two shades that will blend or complement the main color for each bed or border. You can use one color scheme in one area and a different one in another section. Complementary harmony uses two opposite colors, such as orange and blue, or purple and yellow. Analogous harmony uses close colors, such as red with orange and yellow, or blue with violet. Monochromatic harmony uses different tones and shades of the same color, such as you might find in an all-pink garden. (If you're unsure of how to choose colors, you might purchase a color wheel at an art supply store to help you.) White, including white or gray foliage, can be used anywhere, but it is best used for edging. Be careful when using white flowers between colors, for they can have a weak or spotty presence.

Plant Groupings

The impact of your annual border is also determined by the kind of planting you make. A massed planting uses a large bed of one kind of flower in a single color; this approach is quite simple and effective. The mixed bed or border uses plants of different heights and shapes; the tallest flowers grow at the back of the border (or in the middle of a bed), with the lowest-growing ones at the front. In mixed plantings, a combination of different plant shapes is also pleasing; spiked plants work well at the back, rounded plants in the center, and flat-growing plants in front. If you decide to use a mixed planting, don't go overboard—be careful that the arrangement does not look too busy, and plant individual types in groups of three or more for best visual effect.

Formal and Informal Gardens

Whether you plant formal or informal beds and borders depends to a great extent on the style of your house and your personality. Formal beds, which are straight-lined and symmetrical, combine well with Georgian or Greek Revival–style architecture; informal plantings, with curved lines and annuals planted in drifts, complement a woodland cottage or country-style farmhouse.

Preparing the Soil

Once you have decided on the plants you want to grow, and have laid out your plans for the garden, the moment you've waited for—planting—is almost here. Before you pick up your trowel, however, you must be sure that your soil will be a good growing medium; for no matter how high the quality of your plants, they will not flourish if they do not have good soil. In most cases—and especially if there has never been a flower garden in the spot you select—you will have to improve the soil.

Throughout the plant accounts, instructions tell you to plant as soon as the soil can be worked. To test your soil for workability, take a handful and squeeze it into a ball. If the ball remains solid and sticky, the soil is still too wet. Wait a few days and try again. If the soil is very sandy or dusty, water it lightly before working it. When the ball of soil crumbles slightly, the time is right. Do not try to jump the gun and work soil when it is still too wet, for you will only compact it, ruin its texture, and deter your plants' growth. If you are likely to be impatient, you can prepare beds in the fall for planting earlier in the spring.

The first step in improving soil is to dig up any existing grass, weeds, or unwanted plants, and to clear the area of stones and sticks. Then turn your attention to the important qualities of good soil: organic content, drainage, fertilizer, and pH.

Organic Matter and Drainage

Organic matter improves moisture retention, stores nutrients, activates beneficial soil organisms, and aids in drainage. The addition of organic matter will be necessary for growing any annuals except those few that prefer poor soil. The organic matter you add can be peat moss, leaf mold, compost, or dehydrated manure—the choice is not important, so long as organic matter accounts for about 25 percent of the volume in the area where the roots will be growing (approximately the top 8 inches). If a particular plant needs rich soil, the final soil mix should include 30 to 35 percent organic matter.

Soil with a high clay content (called heavy soil) does not drain well and hampers root growth. To improve heavy soil, mix in organic matter or gypsum (calcium sulfate), which you can buy at your local garden center. Sandy soil drains too quickly; incorporate organic matter to help it retain moisture.

Fertilizer

Fertilizer is necessary for good plant growth. Fertilizer comes in different strengths, indicated on the package by a series of three numbers, such as 5–10–5, that tell you the ratio of nitrogen to phosphorus to potassium (N–P–K). When buying fertilizer for annuals, look for a product whose N–P–K ratio is 5–10–5, 10–10–10, or 5–10–10. Normally, you would need 1 to 2 pounds per 100 square feet on a new bed. On established beds, plan to use 1 pound per 100 square feet, unless the results of a soil test advise you otherwise. Follow the directions on the label when applying fertilizer.

Spread the organic matter and fertilizer over the soil and work it in well with a Rototiller or a spade until the soil is uniformly mixed to a depth of at least 8 inches. (Instructions for applying fertilizer throughout the season for established annuals are given in the individual plant accounts.)

The Importance of pH

The pH of a soil indicates its acidity or alkalinity. The pH is measured on a scale of 1 to 14, with 7 being neutral. Most annuals prefer a slightly acid soil, with a pH of 5.5 to 7.0. Check the plant accounts for exceptions. If your soil is too acid, you can raise the pH by adding limestone. Dolomitic limestone is considered best because it is slow to dissolve and will not burn the roots; it also contains magnesium and calcium, elements essential for plant growth. If your soil is too alkaline, you can lower its pH by adding sulfur. If you need to adjust the pH, do so several weeks before you add fertilizer, because the plant nutrients in fertilizers are released only under proper pH conditions.

If you are not sure abut the pH of your soil, don't guess. You can buy a test kit at garden supply stores or have the pH tested by your local Cooperative Extension Service or a soil testing lab (many state universities have such labs). You can also use a test to determine the organic content and nutrient level of the soil if you are unsure about these factors.

Planting Dates

The type of annual you are planting determines the time when it can be planted. Before you make a planting schedule, refer to the frost date map on pages 106–107. The map divides the country into seven areas, based on the average date of the last spring frost and the number of days in the growing season. These dates are, of course, approximations; they can change slightly with your microclimate or fluctuate from year to year with differences in weather.

Do not plant tender annuals before the date given on the map; if you have had a particularly cold spring, wait a little longer. An unexpected late frost could kill tender plants. Half-hardy annuals can generally be planted two to four weeks before the last frost date. Hardy annuals can be planted one to two months before the last frost date. In mild climates, if you are making a planting for fall color, count backwards three months or more from the date of the first fall frost to determine the planting date.

Starting Annuals from Seed

It is easier, especially for beginning gardeners, to buy bedding plants for the annual garden, but many people like to start their own plants from seed. Some varieties of annuals are difficult to buy as plants or are available only from seed catalogs. Seeds may be the only way to get very new and very old species and varieties. Growing from seeds is generally more economical, and it's also a good deal of fun.

Starting Seeds Outdoors

Some annuals cannot be direct-seeded because the seeds are too fine or the growing season is too short; many others, however, grow quickly if planted from seed outdoors. Still others do not transplant well and should be direct seeded for better results.

Before you sow seeds outdoors, prepare the soil in the way described above, then rake it level and moisten it lightly. Directions are given in the plant accounts and on seed packets regarding spacing and planting depth; a general rule of thumb is to sow seeds twice as heavily as the suggested final spacing of the plants, and no deeper than the thickness of the seed.

You can sow seeds in rows or scatter them, depending on your garden design; bear in mind, however, that randomly sown seedlings are often hard to distinguish from weeds. Keep the soil bed evenly moist at all times until the seeds have germinated. Once they sprout, water them daily until the seedlings have four to six leaves and then gradually decrease watering until you can water about once a week.

When the plants are several inches high, they should be thinned to the final spacing given on the seed packet or in the plant accounts in this book. Make sure the soil is moist before thinning and take care not to disturb the roots of the plants that remain. The plants that you take out when thinning the bed can be moved to another bed or given to neighbors.

Starting Seeds Indoors

Annuals that need a head start on the growing season to bloom for the longest possible time, and those whose seeds are very small, should be started indoors. The plant accounts tell you how many weeks of growth the seedlings need before being planted outdoors.

The first thing you need to start seeds indoors is some type of container—which you can purchase or make yourself from milk cartons or aluminum trays. Be sure the container is between 2½ and 4 inches deep, that it has drainage holes, and that it is clean. Before using plastic or metal containers, wash them in a solution of 10 percent chlorine bleach to make sure they are sterile, and rinse them thoroughly. You can also purchase special containers such as peat pots. When sowing seeds, do not reuse a container made of peat or fiber, because these materials may transmit diseases to your seedlings.

The germinating medium is also very important. You can purchase a mixture at your garden center or make your own, using 50 percent fine peat moss and 50 percent fine perlite or vermiculite. Never use garden soil; it is too heavy and contains insects, diseases, and weed seeds.

Fill the container with moistened medium to within ¼ inch of the top and sow the seeds in rows. Small seeds should not be covered during germination, but simply pressed into the surface of the medium. Larger seeds should be covered to a depth about equal their width. Some seeds need darkness to germinate; these are indicated in the plant descriptions. Cover the container with a plastic bag until the seeds germinate. The seeds should not need watering during this period.

Most seeds germinate best if room temperature is about 60° F and the temperature of the medium is 68° to 72° F. Exceptions are discussed in the plant accounts. You can raise the temperature of the medium with heating cables—which you can buy at garden supply stores or through seed catalogs—or by placing the flats in a warm spot, such as on top of the refrigerator. Once the seeds have germinated, the bottom heat is no longer necessary.

There is a disease called "damping off" that kills young seedlings. It can be prevented by using fresh, soilless medium that is not over-watered and by drenching the flat with a fungicide such as benomyl before sowing.

Once the seeds have sprouted, water as soon as the medium starts to dry out. Watering from the bottom is the recommended method, because it will not dislodge small seedlings. When the seedlings have developed two sets of true leaves, thin them so they are about 1 inch apart. Start feeding weekly with one-quarter-strength soluble fertilizer, following the directions on the package.

If you transplant your seedlings into individual cells or pots when they are about 1 inch high, you will make transplanting into the garden easier later on. To avoid burning the tender roots, do not fertilize for two weeks after transplanting.

Grow seedlings on a sunny windowsill or under fluorescent lights; if you grow them under lights, keep them 6 inches above the top of the seedlings and leave them on for 12 to 14 hours a day once the seeds have germinated. Experienced gardeners have found that fluorescent lights give better results than windowsill gardening.

About a week before moving plants into the garden, it is time to start a process called "hardening off," which gradually accustoms seedlings to their new environment. On the first day, move the plants outside into a shaded position out of the wind and bring them back inside at night. Repeat this procedure for several days, and then move the seedlings to a spot where the light they receive will be equivalent to the sunlight in their final home. Leave them outdoors unless a cold night threatens. Plants can also be hardened off in a cold frame, a box with a glass or plastic "skylight" on top.

Buying Annual Plants

When purchasing bedding plants, look for deep green, healthy plants that are neither too compact nor too spindly. Although you will be tempted by flowers, it is better to buy plants that are not yet in bloom. Most annuals will actually come into bloom more quickly if planted green.

If you cannot put your plants out immediately, keep them in a lightly shaded spot and be sure to water them as needed, which may be every day, because the small root balls dry out quickly. Just before planting, water the annuals again, and water the bed into which they will be planted.

Planting

Whether you are planting purchased annuals or home-grown seedlings, the same basic rules apply. To reduce transplanting shock, it is best to put your plants in the ground on a cloudy day or late in the afternoon, if possible. Carefully remove the plants from their cell packs or pots, keeping the root ball intact to avoid damage. The best way to do this is to squeeze or push up the bottom of the container if it is pliable enough, or to turn the container upside down and allow the plant to fall out gently into your hands. The plant should slide out easily if the root ball is moist enough; if not, tap the bottom gently with a trowel. Examine the roots; if they are very compact, loosen them slightly before planting. If you grew your seedlings in peat pots, peel away as much of the pot as possible, and when you plant, be sure the rim of the pot is below the soil surface.

Dig a hole slightly larger than the root ball, set the plant in the ground at the same level at which it was growing in the pot, and carefully firm the soil around the roots. Space the plants according to the instructions in the plant accounts. Water after planting and daily until new growth appears.

Keeping the Garden in Bloom

Once your garden is planted, a regular, but not exhaustive, schedule of maintenance will ensure that it stays at its peak all season. It's a good idea to inspect your plants once a day, so you can spot any problems before they become serious.

Fertilizing

The plant accounts give tips on how often to fertilize. Some annuals prefer an infertile soil, and the fertilizer you added to the ground before planting will be sufficient. Others are heavier feeders and will need fertilizing several times or even monthly. Follow the directions on the fertilizer bag, or provide an estimated 1 pound of 5–10–5 for every 100 square feet every time you fertilize. Soluble fertilizers (a 20–20–20 rating is recommended) are excellent for annuals because they act quickly. If you notice that your plants are producing lush foliage but no flowers, stop fertilizing immediately.

Watering

It is best to water annuals deeply but infrequently—probably weekly—because this practice encourages deep roots. Where temperatures or winds are very high, more frequent watering may be needed. Most annuals like to be watered about as often as the lawn. Exceptions are discussed in the plant accounts.

As you water, keep the leaves as dry as possible to reduce the chance of disease. Soaker hoses, which use less water than overhead sprinkling, also help keep leaves dry. (Overhead watering can also damage blooms.) If you must water overhead, do so in the morning so foliage can dry out before nightfall. If you live in an area with watering restrictions, use drought-resistant annuals, such as celosias, centaureas, California Poppy, and the many others listed in this book.

Mulching and Weeding

After you plant your annuals, add a 2- to 3-inch layer of mulch to conserve soil moisture, cut down on weeds, and keep the soil cool. Organic mulches are the best, and they can be left in place in fall and incorporated into the soil the following spring. Black plastic mulch makes a good barrier against weeds; you can cover it with an organic mulch to make it more attractive.

Weeds compete with annuals for space, food, and water, and harbor insects and diseases. You should remove weeds as soon as possible; weeding is easiest after a rain or watering. There are pre-emergent herbicides that prevent weed seeds from sprouting but do not harm annuals. Consult the experts at your garden center, and follow package directions. Never use any other herbicides in your annual garden.

Dead-heading and Trimming

Some annuals have small flowers that fall cleanly when spent and do not need to be removed. These are good choices for a low-maintenance garden. Larger flowers must be removed as soon as they fade to encourage new growth and flowering and to keep the garden attractive. Removing spent blossoms is known as dead-heading. If plants become too spindly or too large, you may also want to cut them back to keep them tidy.

Winter Cleanup

At the end of the season, after the annuals have been killed by frost, remove the plants from the beds. Those that have shown no signs of disease can be added to the compost pile. The only other "chore" for the winter is to browse through seed catalogs, planning next season's annual garden.

A Note on Plant Names

The common, or English, names of plants are often colorful and evocative: Farewell-to-Spring, Blazing Star, Love-in-a-Mist. But common names vary widely from region to region—Sea Fig and Ice Plant are both names for the same plant. Sometimes, two very different plants may have the same or similar common names, as with German Primrose and Evening Primrose. And some have no comon name at all. But every plant, fortunately, is assigned a scientific, or Latin, name that is distinct and unique to that plant. Scientific names are not necessarily more correct, but they are standard around the world and governed by an international set of rules. Therefore, even though scientific names may at first seem difficult or intimidating, they are in the long run a simple and sure way of distinguishing one plant from another.

A scientific name has two parts. The first is called the generic name; it tells us to which genus (plural, genera) a plant belongs. The second part of the name tells us the species. (A species is a kind of plant or animal that is capable of reproducing with members of its kind but is genetically isolated from others. *Homo sapiens* is a species.) Most genera have many species; *Campanula,* for example, has about 300. *Campanula Medium,* Canterbury Bells, is a species included in this book.

Some scientific names have a third part, which may be in italics or written within single quotation marks in roman type. This third part designates a variety or cultivar; some species may have dozens of varieties or cultivars that differ from the species in plant size, plant form, flower size, or flower color. Technically, a variety is a plant that is naturally produced, while a cultivar (short for "cultivated variety") has been created by a plant breeder. For the purposes of the gardener, they may be treated as the same thing. *Alcea rosea* 'Majorette' is an example.

A hybrid is a plant that is the result of a cross between two genera, two species, or two varieties or cultivars. Sometimes hybrids are given a new scientific name, but they are usually indicated by an × within the scientific name: *Pelargonium* × *domesticum,* Martha Washington Geranium, is a hybrid in this book.

Organization of the Plant Accounts

The plant accounts in this book are arranged alphabetically by scientific name. If you know only the common name of a flower, refer to the index and turn to the page given.

Some accounts in the book deal with a garden plant at the genus level—because the genus includes many similar species that can be treated in more or less the same way in the garden. In these accounts, only the genus name is given at the top of the page; the name of the species, cultivar, or hybrid pictured is given within the text.

One Last Word

Whether you are interested in annuals for borders, beds, ground covers, rock gardens, containers, or cutting, these tips and the information in the plant accounts that follow will show you exactly how to grow them to perfection.

Annuals

Common Garden Ageratum
(Ageratum Houstonianum)

Tender

For borders, edgings, and container plantings in shades of true blue (as well as a handful of pink or white varieties), few annuals beat Ageratum, or Flossflower, as it is also known. From early summer until frost, clusters of tiny, fluffy flowers that look like powder-puffs bloom nonstop. The blooms cover the compact plants, most of which grow 4–8 inches high and have a mounded habit. The leaves are heart shaped. The cultivar 'North Sea' is shown here.

GROWING TIPS

Although Ageratum seeds can be sown outdoors, you will have better results using purchased plants or starting seeds indoors 6–8 weeks before the last frost. Seeds need light to germinate, so don't cover them. Set plants outdoors after the last frost, 6–8 inches apart, in sun or light shade. Ageratum is not fussy about soil, but does better in soil that is rich, moist, and well drained. Water Ageratum when the ground starts to dry out and fertilize monthly; other than that Ageratum needs little care.

Garden Hollyhock *(Alcea rosea)* Hardy

We remember hollyhocks as the tall, stately plants growing 4–6 feet high along the fences in Grandmother's garden. But there are also varieties of hollyhock that grow only 2 feet tall. Both the tall and short varieties have stiff spikes of papery, single or double flowers in a wide range of colors. The dwarf form 'Majorette', pictured, has double flowers. Use hollyhocks as accent plants or at backs of borders.

GROWING TIPS

Some hollyhocks are perennials or biennials; others are true annuals. Buy plants or start seeds indoors 6–8 weeks before the last frost, because seeds started outdoors may never grow into blooming plants. Set plants out after the last frost, in full sun or light shade, 18–24 inches apart. Soil should be rich and well drained. Hollyhocks like to be watered heavily and fertilized monthly. They self-sow readily, but the resulting plants are usually inferior. If you grow the taller varieties, be prepared to stake them.

Common Snapdragon *(Antirrhinum majus)* Half-hardy

The flowers of old-fashioned snapdragons snap tightly over your finger if you insert it into the bloom. Today, the traditional forms have been joined by open-faced and double blooms. The showy spikes of flowers have a light, spicy fragrance and come in a wide range of colors except clear blue. Dwarf snaps grow only 6–8 inches high; there are also intermediate sizes and tall classics reaching 3 feet. Depending on their size, snapdragons work well in borders, beds, or rock gardens. They also make good cut flowers.

GROWING TIPS

Snapdragon seeds can be sown outdoors in mid-spring after the soil has started to warm up, but you will get better results if you buy seedlings or start seeds indoors 6–8 weeks before planting. The plants tolerate light frost and can be put in the garden early. Space them 6–15 inches apart, depending on their mature height, in full sun or light shade, pinching young plants to encourage more flowers. They grow best in fertile soil that is moist and well drained. Cut flowers as they fade to encourage continued bloom.

African Daisy *(Arctotis stoechadifolia)*

Originally, African Daisies (also called Blue-eyed Daisies) had daisy-shaped, 3-inch flowers with blue-violet centers and petals of creamy yellow with reddish undersides. They grew 2½–4 feet high over a mound of woolly, whitish leaves. The African Daisy hybrids available today are lower growing, reaching 10–12 inches in height, and have flowers in all colors but blue. Flowers bloom all summer, but they close up at night, so plant them in beds and borders planned for daytime viewing.

GROWING TIPS

Sow African Daisy seeds outdoors in late spring after all danger of frost has passed or start with purchased seedlings or start seeds indoors 6–8 weeks earlier. Set plants 12 inches apart in full sun. African Daisy likes poor, dry, sandy soil with excellent drainage; do not over-water, and fertilize sparingly if at all. African Daisy grows best where nights are cool; it can be used as a spring or fall annual in hot areas. To extend the flowering period, and to keep plants tidy, pick off faded flowers.

Wax Begonia *(Begonia × semperflorens-cultorum)* Tender

Sometimes called Fibrous Begonias because of the texture of their roots, Wax Begonias have neat mounds of round foliage and small single or double flowers that are white, pink, rose, or red. The plants grow 6–12 inches high and are covered with waxy leaves of green, bronze, or brown. There are many varieties; 'Gin' is shown here. Everblooming, they are spectacular in beds or as tidy edgings.

GROWING TIPS

If you want to grow Wax Begonias from seed—a challenge even for the experts—start them indoors 12–16 weeks before the last frost. Seeds are fine, dusty, and difficult to handle; it is much easier to start from purchased plants. Once frost danger has passed, set plants outdoors, 6–8 inches apart, in partial shade. In hot areas, use the heat-resistant bronze-leaved varieties. Soil should be rich and well drained; Wax Begonias will tolerate dry conditions between waterings. Feed once a month for most vigorous growth.

English Daisy *(Bellis perennis)*

Half-hardy

Technically perennials or biennials that bloom in the spring, English Daisies are often grown as annuals, in which case they bloom in the summer. The daisylike flowers come in white, pink, and red, with a bright yellow center. They may be single or double and are 1–2 inches across. They appear on 4- to 6-inch stems over a tufted rosette of leaves. Because of their petite size, English Daisies work best in low borders, as edgings, and in rock gardens.

GROWING TIPS

If you are growing English Daisy as an annual, start seeds indoors 8–10 weeks before the planting date. Seedlings can be moved to the garden several weeks before the last spring frost, since they don't mind a little chill. English Daisy prefers cool climates; in hot areas, it should be grown in spring or fall. Space plants 6 inches apart in full sun or light shade. They do best in light soil that is fertile and well watered. English Daisies can become weedy from dropped seeds; remove flowers as soon as they fade.

Ornamental Kale (Brassica oleracea)

Hardy

The fall and winter garden needn't be without color. Ornamental Kale and Cabbage (*B. oleracea*, Acephala Group) have open rosettes of green leaves with centers of white, pink, and purple that show their best color after they have been nipped by frost. Growing up to 12–15 inches across and 10 inches high, these plants make an unusual and decorative accent or massed planting in fall and winter.

GROWING TIPS

Cool temperatures are the key to growing Ornamental Kale and Cabbage. Plan on adding plants to the garden about 1 month before the first expected fall frost. Color starts to develop at 50° F and intensifies with frost. You can buy plants or start seeds indoors 6–8 weeks before planting time. Space plants 12–15 inches apart in full sun and fertile soil that is moist and well drained. In areas where winter temperatures do not drop below 20° F, Ornamental Kale and Cabbage will last for months.

Browallia *(Browallia speciosa)*

Half-hardy

With its long stems and many flowers cascading over the sides, Browallia is a good choice for containers and hanging baskets. Stems grow from 8–18 inches long and are clothed in velvety, star- to bell-shaped, 2-inch flowers that are white, blue, or purple. The violet-blue variety 'Blue Bells' is shown here. *B. viscosa* is a similar plant that tends to flower more heavily.

GROWING TIPS

Do not attempt to start Browallia seeds outdoors; you will have little if any success. Instead, buy plants or start seeds indoors 6–8 weeks before the outdoor planting date. Don't cover the seeds; they need light to germinate. Browallia can withstand light frosts, so move the plants to the garden about 2 weeks before the last expected spring frost. Set them 6–10 inches apart in partial shade and rich, well-drained soil. Heavy fertilizing is unnecessary; keep the soil cool and moist with a summer mulch.

Pot Marigold *(Calendula officinalis)*

Hardy

Whether in containers or massed beds, the bright, 3- to 4-inch blooms of Pot Marigold are smashing. The crisp, daisylike flowers are single or double and either cream, yellow, gold, apricot, or orange; 'Orange Coronet' is shown here. Depending on the variety, Pot Marigolds grow from 6–24 inches high. Early herbalists, who grew these flowers as culinary and medicinal herbs, thought they were marigolds—hence the name.

GROWING TIPS

Pot Marigold seeds can be started indoors 4–6 weeks before the outside planting date or sown directly into the garden about 4 weeks before the last frost. The plants themselves can go outside 2 weeks before the last frost. They prefer full sun but will grow in partial shade. Space them 12–15 inches apart in fertile soil that is moist and well drained. Pot Marigolds do best when it is below 80° F; grow them in spring or fall in hot areas. Cut flowers off as they fade to keep plants neat and encourage continued bloom.

China Aster *(Callistephus chinensis)* Tender

China Asters come in many different flower forms, including chrysanthemum, pompon, plumed, peony, and cactus. Blooms begin in midsummer. Depending on the variety, the flowers measure 2–4 inches across and the plants range from 6–36 inches high. 'Early Charm Choice', shown here, is an early bloomer. Blooms, which may be single or double, are white, pink, red, yellow, lavender, purple, or blue. China Aster is a good plant for beds and borders; the flowers are excellent for cutting.

GROWING TIPS

You can start China Asters from either seeds or purchased plants. Sow seeds outdoors after all danger of frost has passed or indoors 6–8 weeks before the planting date. Set plants into the garden after the last frost, spacing them 6–15 inches apart, depending on their mature size. Give them full sun and fertile soil that is moist and well drained. Mulch in summer to keep the roots moist. Once a plant has bloomed, it will not rebloom, so add plants every 2 weeks to ensure continuous flowering.

Canterbury Bells *(Campanula Medium)* Hardy

This group of bellflowers is a large one, with many perennial and biennial relatives. Canterbury Bells, biennials grown as annuals, have 1- to 2-inch, bell-shaped flowers of white, blue, lavender, or pink that bloom in summer. The plants grow 2–3 feet tall. Because of their height, Canterbury Bells are used as accent plants or at the back of the border; they make long-lasting cut flowers as well.

Growing Tips

Canterbury Bells grow and flower best when it is cool. Plants can be added to the garden in mid-spring, spaced 12–15 inches apart. If you want to start plants from seeds, they must be sown indoors 6–8 weeks before outdoor planting time. In warm climates, seeds sown in the garden in the fall will germinate the following spring. Canterbury Bells like full sun or light shade and rich, moist, well-drained soil. Clip off faded flowers to encourage continued bloom; fertilize monthly while the plants are flowering.

Madagascar Periwinkle *(Catharanthus roseus)* Tender

Also known as Vinca (but not to be confused with the perennial ground cover *Vinca*), Madagascar Periwinkle has leathery leaves and waxy, 1-inch-wide flowers. The 5-petaled flowers are white, pink, or rose, and sometimes have a pink or red center. The white variety 'Albus' is shown here. Some varieties are spreading and low-growing, reaching only 3–5 inches high, while others grow upright to 12 inches high. Madagascar Periwinkle tolerates heat, drought, and air pollution, and its waxy leaves shed dust and dirt.

Growing Tips

Set Madagascar Periwinkle plants into the garden after all frost danger has passed. If you want to grow your own plants, start seeds indoors 12 weeks before the planting date. Spacing of Madagascar Periwinkle depends on plant habit; low-growing varieties need about 24 inches, while upright ones may be spaced about 6 inches apart. Give plants full sun or partial shade and average, well-drained soil. Faded flowers fall cleanly and need not be removed.

Celosia *(Celosia cristata)*

Tender

Celosia is an eye-catcher; the two forms and the many colors of its flowers are striking. Plumed Celosia has long, feathery flower stalks; pictured is the variety 'Century Mixed'. Crested Celosia, or Cockscomb, has round, ridged flowers that resemble a brain or the comb of a rooster. Both types come in bright shades of red, rose, pink, yellow, cream, apricot, orange, gold, and salmon. Dwarf Celosias grow 6 inches high; tall varieties reach 2½ feet. *C. cristata* is sometimes sold as *C. plumosa.*

GROWING TIPS

Move Celosia plants into the garden after all danger of frost has passed and space them 6–18 inches apart. If you set out plants too early, cool weather can cause them to set seed prematurely, and they will have to be replaced. Celosias should be planted before they are in bloom. Give them full sun and rich, well-drained soil; do not fertilize. Celosia is very tolerant of heat and drought and will add color to the garden until frost.

Centaurea *(Centaurea)*

The *Centaurea* species are primarily blue or violet, but there are also pink and white varieties. Basket-Flower *(C. americana)*, pictured here, looks like a flower set into a basket. It grows 4 feet tall and has 4- to 5-inch, violet or pink flowers. Bachelor's Button *(C. cyanus)*, also known as Cornflower, usually grows 12–24 inches high, depending on the variety. Its flowers are double, frilled, ruffled, or tufted, and usually blue, though they also come in pink or white.

GROWING TIPS

Basket-Flowers and Bachelor's Buttons are very frost hardy and can be planted in early spring to mid-spring as soon as the soil can be worked. For early bloom, start with purchased plants or sow seeds indoors 4 weeks before the planting date. Where winters are mild, sow seeds in fall for spring bloom. Centaureas are not long-blooming; set out new plants every 2 weeks for continuous bloom. Set plants 6–24 inches apart in full sun and rich or poor soil. Centaureas prefer dry soil and tolerate drought.

Chrysanthemum (*Chrysanthemum*) Hardy

The chrysanthemum, the favorite perennial of the fall, has a number of annual cousins that can brighten up summer borders and beds. Tricolor Chrysanthemum, *C. carinatum* ('Merry Mixture' is shown here), is 2–3 feet high and has deeply cut foliage. Flowers, which are single or double, are white, red, gold, yellow, or purple, with contrasting rings. Crown Daisy, *C. coronarium,* is a neat, 1½- to 2-foot, dome-shaped plant with fernlike foliage and buttonlike double flowers in gold or yellow.

GROWING TIPS

Set chrysanthemum seeds or plants into the garden in mid-spring, about 4 weeks before the last frost. In hot areas, mums do not do well in midsummer, but seeds can be resown in summer for a bright fall display. Set plants 1–2 feet apart, in full sun and well-drained soil. Fertilize monthly and keep flowers picked to ensure continuous blooming. Although they do better where summers are mild and moist, annual chrysanthemums tolerate a moderate amount of heat and drought.

Farewell-to-Spring *(Clarkia amoena)*

Hardy

Farewell-to-Spring's pretty, light-hearted appearance makes it at home in the wildflower or natural-istic garden. It can also be used in beds and borders and makes a good cut flower. The single or double flowers are delicate, showy, satiny, and sometimes frilled; they bloom in spikes on 1- to 3-foot stems. Flower colors range from white through pink, red, lavender, and purple. Some blooms are blotched in contrasting colors.

GROWING TIPS

Sow *Clarkia* seeds directly into the garden; they rarely grow well in-doors. They may be sown in early spring as soon as the soil can be worked; in mild areas, sow in the fall for germination the following spring. Space seedlings 8–10 inches apart; crowding them together in-creases blooming. *Clarkia* likes full sun or light shade and light, sandy soil with excellent drainage. Water very lightly and do not fertilize, or you will have lush foliage but no flowers. Farewell-to-Spring grows best where nights are cool.

Spider Flower *(Cleome Hasslerana)* Half-hardy

Spider Flower's large blooms have 4 long-clawed petals and characteristically long stamens. The 6- to 7-inch flowers are strongly scented and may be white, rose, pink, or lavender. After the flowers fade, long, slim, conspicuous seedpods form. The foliage is compound, with 5–7 fingerlike leaflets and 2 spines at the base of each leaf. Spider Flower is most attractive in clumps at the back of a border or bed, where the 3- to 6-foot stems can sway in summer breezes.

GROWING TIPS

Plant Spider Flower seeds or plants in the garden after all danger of frost has passed. If you want to get a head start with your seeds, start them indoors 4–6 weeks before the last frost. Space plants 2–3 feet apart in average soil and full sun. Spider Flower likes summer warmth and withstands high heat and drought. Feed very lightly, if at all, and don't over-water. Staking is usually not necessary.

Garden Coleus *(Coleus × hybridus)*

Tender

Coleus is much admired for its foliage, which comes in splashy combinations of green, yellow, white, gold, red, orange, purple, and pink. The leaves are edged, blotched, or patterned in contrasting colors and have lacy, smooth, fringed, wavy, or toothed margins. Coleus develops thin spikes of blue flowers in late summer, but it is grown mainly for its foliage. Depending on the variety, it grows from 8–24 inches high. If you need an annual to brighten the shade, Coleus does the job in beds, borders, or containers.

GROWING TIPS

Set Coleus plants into the garden after frost danger has passed, using either purchased plants or plants started from seeds indoors 6–8 weeks earlier. Seeds need light to germinate, so don't cover them. Coleus can also be propagated easily from cuttings. Set plants 10–12 inches apart in partial to heavy shade and moist soil that is well drained and moderately fertile. If Coleus receives too much sun, the foliage will fade. Pick flowers as they form to extend the period of bright foliage color.

Rocket Larkspur *(Consolida ambigua)* Hardy

Related to the perennial delphiniums, Rocket Larkspur has similar 1- to 3-foot spikes clothed with 1- to 3-inch flowers of white, blue, purple, pink, and lavender. Foliage is narrow and finely divided. Rocket Larkspur is sometimes featured in watercolors of old-fashioned gardens, but it is still useful today for backgrounds, borders, or as a cut flower. Larkspur prefers cool weather, so blooms are usually at their best in spring and early summer. Rocket Larkspur is sometimes sold as *Delphinium Ajacis.*

GROWING TIPS

Sow Rocket Larkspur seeds in the garden in early spring as soon as the soil can be worked; in mild areas, sow seeds in fall for early spring flowers. (You can start seeds indoors 6–8 weeks before outdoor planting, but larkspur does not transplant well.) Space the plants 12–36 inches apart and give them a spot in full sun. They grow best in rich, loose soil that is slightly alkaline. Fertilize at planting time and again monthly. To extend the bloom, pick flowers as they fade. Mulch to keep the soil cool and moist.

Garden Cosmos *(Cosmos bipinnatus)* Tender

Cosmos fill the garden with light, airy clusters of single or double, daisylike flowers that bloom on bushy, 3- to 4-foot plants. The petals are wide and serrated and may be white, pink, rose, or lavender. Stems are slender, carrying 3- to 6-inch blooms nonstop from early summer until frost. The foliage is lacy. Cosmos are excellent plants for the back of the border, for large massed plantings, or for cut flowers.

GROWING TIPS

Cosmos seeds can be sown outdoors where plants are to grow after all danger of frost has passed; for earlier bloom, buy plants or start seeds inside 5–7 weeks earlier. Space Cosmos plants 1½–2 feet apart in a warm, sunny spot. Cosmos do best in dry, poor, sandy soil; rich soil produces lots of leaves but no flowers. Do not fertilize Cosmos, and water them very sparingly. To keep the plants tidy, cut off flowers as they fade.

Dahlia Hybrids (*Dahlia*) Tender

Some dahlias grown by hobbyists reach up to 6 feet in height and have flowers the size of dinner plates; there are also low-growing dahlias quite at home as bedding plants in the flower garden. Bedding dahlias grow 8–12 inches tall. They have flowers in all colors but blue and may be single, double, or fancy in form. Almost all dahlia mixes come in a variety of colors, and you won't know what colors you will have until they bloom. Flowering all summer, dahlias are excellent plants for massed beds, borders, and containers.

GROWING TIPS

Set dahlia plants into the garden after all danger of frost has passed; use purchased plants or plants started from seeds indoors 4–6 weeks earlier. Dahlias like a spot with full sun or light shade and light, fertile soil with excellent drainage. Space plants 6 inches apart, fertilizing at planting time and again monthly. Water heavily and mulch plants to keep the soil moist. Dahlias produce tubers that can be dug up and stored over the winter, but it's just as easy to start new plants from seed each year.

Sweet William *(Dianthus barbatus)*

Hardy

Sweet William is a biennial often grown as an annual. The attractive plants grow to 15 inches high and are topped with clusters of red, white, pink, rose, or lilac flowers. The flowers have a clovelike fragrance and are slightly fringed around the edges. Sweet William can be grown in containers or as a border or rock garden plant.

GROWING TIPS
Buy Sweet William plants in spring or start seeds indoors 6–8 weeks before the planting date. Set plants outdoors after all danger of frost has passed. Space them 6–8 inches apart in full sun or light shade. They grow best in light, rich, well-drained soil; add lime if the soil is too acidic. Fertilize at planting time and again monthly while the plants are growing and flowering. Cut plants back after they bloom to encourage more flowers. Sweet William grows best where nights are cool and humidity is high.

China Pink (*Dianthus chinensis*)

Half-hardy

China Pinks (or Indian Pinks) did not get their name because the flowers are pink, but because their serrated edges look like they were cut with pinking shears. The blooms are usually pink but can also be white, red, or lilac, with a contrasting center. 'Telestar Mix' is shown here. China Pinks grow 6–18 inches tall and are topped by flat clusters of fragrant flowers in early summer. Some varieties continue to bloom well into summer, especially if the weather is cool.

GROWING TIPS

Place China Pink plants in the garden in spring after all danger of frost has passed. Seeds can be started indoors 6–8 weeks before outdoor planting time; in mild areas, sow seeds outdoors in fall for spring bloom. Plant China Pinks in full sun or light shade. They prefer rich, slightly alkaline soil that is moist and well drained. Cut off flowers as soon as they fade to prolong the blooming time. China Pinks will sometimes survive the winter, returning to bloom in spring and early summer.

Annual Foxglove *(Digitalis purpurea)*

Annual Foxgloves, which can grow up to 6 feet tall, are dramatic plants with spikes of nodding, 1- to 3-inch, bell-shaped flowers. The blooms are white, yellow, pink, purple, or red, and many are spotted with a contrasting color on the inside. The variety 'Foxy' is pictured. Annual Foxgloves can be used as bold accent plants or in the middle or back of a flower border. They bloom most abundantly in late spring and early summer and may bloom longer if the climate is cool and the faded flowers are picked off. Foxglove is toxic if eaten.

GROWING TIPS

Although they are biennials, these foxgloves can be grown as annuals if plants are put in the garden 2 weeks before the last spring frost. If you are going to start your own plants from seed, start them indoors 10–12 weeks before transplanting time. Foxgloves like partial shade and rich, loose, well-drained soil. Space plants 15–24 inches apart, fertilizing them at planting time and again when they bloom. Water well; never allow the soil to dry out. Foxglove does not grow well in excessive heat. It easily reseeds.

Cape Marigold *(Dimorphotheca pluvialis)*   Tender

Cheerful-looking annuals, Cape Marigolds are a bright addition to a bed or border. They grow 16 inches high and are graced with 2½-inch, daisylike flowers. The blooms are white, with violet to purple undersides and yellow centers. They close up at night. The leaves are lance shaped and cleft with jagged lobes.

GROWING TIPS

Cape Marigold is a tender annual that prefers cool growing conditions. Set plants or sow seeds into the garden after all danger of frost has passed, finally spacing them 6–8 inches apart. For early bloom, start seeds indoors 4–5 weeks before the last frost. Cape Marigold likes full sun and light, sandy, well-drained soil. Water lightly—it prefers dry soil—and fertilize every other month. While Cape Marigold enjoys cool weather, it will tolerate some heat and drought.

Livingstone Daisy *(Dorotheanthus bellidiformis)* Tender

A low-growing succulent, Livingstone Daisy looks at first like a small rock or stone. Suddenly, these rocks open into bright, showy, daisylike flowers of pink, red, white, or orange—this transformation accounts for the common name. When in bloom, these spreading plants are 3 inches high; flowers are 2 inches across. Livingstone Daisy is a perennial in the warm South and West, where it is a popular ground cover. Elsewhere, it is grown as an annual. It is a good plant for the seashore because it tolerates salt spray.

GROWING TIPS
Plant Livingstone Daisy in full sun after the last spring frost, spacing plants 2–6 inches apart. Seeds should be started indoors, 10–12 weeks before outdoor planting time; cover the flats with black plastic until seeds sprout, because the seeds need darkness to germinate. Livingstone Daisy tolerates poor to average soil as long as it is dry. Fertilize at planting time and again every other month while the plant is growing and flowering.

Dahlberg Daisy (*Dyssodia tenuiloba*)

Half-hardy

From a distance, Dahlberg Daisy looks like bright flecks of gold on a low, dark, dense carpet. Growing about 6–12 inches tall, Dahlberg Daisy forms dense mounds of fine, threadlike leaves on slender stems. The yellow to yellow-orange, daisylike flowers are 1 inch across and single. Besides making a good ground cover, Dahlberg Daisy does well as a low border or edging plant or in a rock garden. It is sometimes called *Thymophylla tenuiloba*.

GROWING TIPS

Buy Dahlberg Daisy plants, or start seeds indoors 6–8 weeks before the last spring frost, and transplant them outdoors after all danger of frost has passed. Set plants 4–6 inches apart, in full sun and average garden soil with good drainage. They grow best in dry soil, so water sparingly. Little if any fertilizer is needed. Dahlberg Daisy prefers cool temperatures but tolerates heat and drought well.

California Poppy *(Eschscholzia californica)*   Hardy

California Poppy is the state flower of California. Its silky flowers are 2–3 inches across, cup shaped, and either single or double. Many have crinkled petals. California Poppy's colors include gold, yellow, bronze, scarlet, rose, or white. The flower stems grow 12–24 inches high, above finely divided, silver-gray, spreading foliage. California Poppy is useful as a wildflower and also grows well in borders, massed plantings, and containers. The flowers close up at night.

Growing Tips

California Poppies do not transplant well, so starting seeds indoors is not recommended. Sow seeds outdoors in early spring where they are to grow, in a spot with full sun and light, sandy, well-drained soil. Soil should be poor and infertile; add no organic matter and do not fertilize. Thin plants to 6–8 inches apart. California Poppy is tolerant of heat and drought. In mild climates, it self-sows readily and acts as a perennial. It is used in warm areas as a source of color in fall, winter, and spring.

Lisianthus *(Eustoma grandiflorum)*   Half-hardy

While Lisianthus, also known as Prairie Gentian and Bluebell, is not a new plant, it is relatively unfamiliar to most gardeners. Perhaps best known as a cut flower lasting up to 14 days, Lisianthus grows well in beds, borders, or pots. It has single or double, 3-inch flowers of pink, white, blue, or lavender. Blooms are cup shaped, facing upward, and appear in clusters. Lisianthus plants can grow 30 inches tall, but if kept to 12 inches they will be stronger and flower more. Lisianthus is also sold as *Lisianthus Russellianus.*

GROWING TIPS

It takes 7 months from the time Lisianthus seeds are sown until plants bloom, so starting seeds indoors may not be practical. Instead, purchase plants and set them into the garden, spaced 12 inches apart, after the last spring frost. Give plants a warm spot with full sun or light shade; they will tolerate dry or moist garden soil, as long as it is well drained. Fertilize at planting time and again every other month. Pinch Lisianthus as soon as it is planted and again when 2–3 inches of new growth has developed.

Blanket Flower *(Gaillardia pulchella)*

Half-hardy

The blooms of Blanket Flower, or Indian Blanket, come in a brilliant color range of reds, bronzes, maroons, and golds. Petals are fringed and tipped in yellow. The ball-shaped flowers are double, growing 2½ inches across. The plants are trim and mounded, grow 10–24 inches high, and are covered with flowers from early summer to frost. There are many cultivars; 'Gaiety' is pictured. Most often used in beds and borders, Blanket Flower also makes a good cut flower.

GROWING TIPS

You can sow Blanket Flower seeds in the garden after all danger of frost has passed or, for early bloom, buy plants or start your own plants indoors 4–6 weeks before planting time. Space plants 12–24 inches apart, depending on their mature height (plant them as far apart as they will grow tall). Blanket Flower grows best in hot, full sun and dry, light, open soil that is well drained. Fertilize little if at all; it likes poor, infertile soil. To keep plants neat, remove flowers as they fade.

Treasure Flower (*Gazania rigens*) Tender

Treasure Flower has single, daisylike blooms. Most varieties are solid colored, in tones of yellow, gold, orange, cream, pink, or red, but others are interestingly striped. Many have contrasting centers of yellow or black. The flowers, depending on the variety, are 2–5 inches across. They bloom on 8- to 10-inch stems over a mat of basal foliage. Leaves are dark green on top and felty white on the undersides. The flowers close at night and on cloudy days. Use Treasure Flower as a ground cover or an edging plant.

GROWING TIPS
Add Treasure Flower seeds or plants to the garden after the last spring frost. To get a head start on blooms, you can start seeds indoors 4–6 weeks earlier. Set plants 8–10 inches apart, in full sun and light, sandy soil with excellent drainage. Fertilize at planting time; no further feeding is necessary. Treasure Flower does best where summer temperatures are high; it also tolerates drought. Cut flowers as they fade to encourage more blooms and to keep plants tidy.

Transvaal Daisy *(Gerbera Jamesonii)*

Half-hardy

Transvaal Daisy bears large, 5-inch flowers on thick stems in bright shades of orange, red, pink, white, yellow, salmon, or lavender. The cultivar 'Happipot' is shown here. The leafless flower stalks, 6–12 inches tall, rise above dark green, ground-hugging foliage with white, fuzzy undersides. An excellent plant in beds, borders, or containers, Transvaal Daisy also makes a long-lasting cut flower. The plants will bloom for about 2 months.

GROWING TIPS

You can usually find pots of Transvaal Daisies at garden centers in the spring. The plants can be added to the garden after all danger of frost has passed. (If you want to grow Transvaal Daisies from seeds, you will have to start them indoors 6 months earlier.) Space the plants 12–15 inches apart in full sun; they prefer a moist, rich, slightly acid soil. Do not plant too deeply, or the plants will rot. Feed plants monthly when they are in bloom and remove faded flowers. Transvaal Daisy is a perennial in warm climates.

Sunflower *(Helianthus annuus)*

You may rightly think of sunflowers as tall, coarse plants with large, hairy, sticky leaves and giant golden flowers. Today, however, there are also varieties that grow only 12–15 inches tall, compared to the 4- to 12-foot heights some varieties attain. Regardless of height, sunflowers bear large, daisy-like flowers in many shades of yellow, as well as white, orange, and maroon. Some have contrasting centers of brown; some have double blooms. Sunflower seeds, which are edible and nutritious, attract birds to the garden.

GROWING TIPS

Sunflowers grow very fast from seed, so there is no need to start them indoors, although you can do so if you like. Plant seeds 1–2 weeks before last frost, or seedlings after all danger of frost has passed, in full sun and light, dry, well-drained soil. Space plants 1–4 feet apart, depending on their ultimate size. Do not fertilize them, and water them very little. Sunflowers grow best in hot climates.

Strawflower *(Helichrysum bracteatum)*

Half-hardy

The brightly colored blooms of Strawflower come in shades of red, orange, purple, yellow, pink, or white. The flowers, which are actually bracts, are stiff and papery. Strawflowers are usually grown as a source of flowers for drying—their other common name is Everlasting —but they are nonetheless quite attractive in beds and borders. Their stems are narrow and wiry, usually growing 12–30 inches high. There are several dwarf forms, including 'Bikini', shown here, growing less than 12 inches tall.

GROWING TIPS

You may sow Strawflower seeds in the garden after all danger of frost has passed, but you will have better success if you use bedding plants or start seeds indoors 4–6 weeks earlier. Strawflower likes full sun and loose, well-drained, dry soil. Fertilize every 2 weeks during the growing season. Strawflower grows best where summers are hot and dry. To dry the flowers, cut them just before the central petals open, strip off the foliage, and hang them upside down in a shaded area.

Common Heliotrope *(Heliotropium arborescens)* Tender

In zones 9–10, where it is a perennial, Heliotrope grows 4–6 feet tall. In other areas, where it is grown as an annual, it reaches 2 feet high. Heliotrope flowers grow in flat, 6- to 8-inch clusters over dark, textured foliage. Tiny white, dark blue, or purple flowers bloom all summer long; 'Marine' is pictured. Heliotrope is highly fragrant and should be placed where its scent can be enjoyed.

GROWING TIPS

To grow Heliotrope, start with purchased plants or with plants started indoors 10–12 weeks before outdoor planting time. It is very sensitive to frost, so don't put plants into the garden until 2 weeks after the last spring frost date. Space Heliotrope plants 12 inches apart in full sun. They will grow in average garden soil but will do better in soil that is rich and well drained. Water frequently so the soil never dries out. In hot areas Heliotrope benefits from afternoon shade.

Rose Mallow *(Hibiscus moscheutos)*

Half-hardy

For a touch of the exotic, use Rose Mallow in your garden as a specimen plant or a hedge. Although it is actually a perennial, Rose Mallow is usually grown as an annual. The plants, depending on the variety, grow from 1½–6 feet high. Flowers range in size from 4–10 inches across and in color from rose, red, and pink to white or cream, often with a contrasting eye. Most Rose Mallow flowers are single and have a large, prominent tubelike structure projecting from the center.

GROWING TIPS

Add Rose Mallow plants to the garden after all danger of frost has passed in spring. It is best to use purchased plants; seeds sown outdoors will never develop into blooming plants. Sown indoors, seeds need 3 months of growth before they can be planted outside. If you do start with seeds, nick the hard coat before sowing. Space plants 18–36 inches apart in full sun or light shade and rich, moist, well-drained soil. Rose Mallow tolerates heat if it is well watered. Fertilize only at planting time.

Mexican Tulip Poppy
(Hunnemannia fumariifolia)

Half-hardy

This native of Mexico looks like a cross between a tulip and a poppy, which is how it got its common name. The rich yellow blooms are 3 inches across and have a wavy edge. The bluish-green leaves covering the 1- to 2-foot plant are soft, smooth, and finely divided. Mexican Tulip Poppy, which makes a good cut flower, is a pretty flower for the border, blooming all summer long.

GROWING TIPS

Plant Mexican Tulip Poppy seeds or purchased plants outdoors after all danger of frost has passed. The roots do not like to be disturbed, so transplant carefully. If you start your own plants from seeds, sow them in individual pots so they won't be disturbed and give them 4–6 weeks growing time indoors. Set plants 9–12 inches apart in full sun. They prefer a warm, light, dry soil that is well drained and slightly alkaline. Feed Mexican Tulip Poppy little if any and water it very lightly.

Candytuft *(Iberis)*

Two different candytufts can be grown in the summer garden. Rocket Candytuft, *I. amara,* grows 12–18 inches tall and is covered with large, upright, cone-shaped spikes of fragrant, shiny, white flowers. It is excellent as a cut flower. Globe Candytuft, *I. umbellata* (pictured), is a dome-shaped, slightly spreading plant, growing 8–12 inches high. The flowers are pink, crimson, rose, red, lavender, or white; they have no fragrance.

GROWING TIPS

For earliest bloom, buy bedding plants, or start candytuft seeds indoors 6–8 weeks before planting time. Candytuft seeds can be sown outdoors, but they will not develop into large, strong plants before summer's heat, except in cooler climates. Set the plants into the garden after frost danger has passed. Space them 6–10 inches apart in full sun and average, well-drained soil. Fertilize at planting time; water only when the soil is dry. After flowers fade, shear plants to encourage further bloom.

ANNUALS **63**

Impatiens *(Impatiens Wallerana)* Tender

Winning all popularity polls, this impatiens (also known as Busy Lizzy and Patience Plant) is well loved for its various colors and sizes, its dependability, and its non-stop bloom until frost. These shade-tolerant plants grow 4–18 inches tall, depending on the variety. Flowers are white, pink, salmon, orange, scarlet, red, and violet. Most flowers are flat, 1–2 inches across, and have 5 petals, although there are also double-flowered forms. *Impatiens* 'New Guinea', a relative, is grown more for its variegated foliage than its flowers.

GROWING TIPS

Add impatiens plants to the shady bed or border after all danger of frost has passed. If you want to grow your own plants from seeds, you will have to start them indoors 10–14 weeks earlier. Impatiens can also be increased from cuttings. Plant them 10–18 inches apart in rich, slightly moist soil and partial to full shade. Do not over-water impatiens, and feed them very lightly or the plants will not flower. New Guinea Impatiens prefers full sun and moist, cool soil.

Standing Cypress *(Ipomopsis rubra)*

Standing Cypress flowers are unique and eye-catching; they are long, slim tubes opening into 5-pointed stars at the tip. The blooms are red on the outside with red and yellow speckles on the inside. The plants, which can grow up to 6 feet high (but usually reach only 3 feet), are covered in dainty, feathery leaves. Use Standing Cypress in the back of the border or as an accent plant or hedge.

GROWING TIPS

Standing Cypress is a biennial but can be grown as an annual if it is started early enough. Sow seeds outdoors in early spring as soon as the soil can be worked. Seeds sown in late summer will flower the following year. You can start seeds indoors if the temperature in your house is cool, but Standing Cypress does not transplant well. Space plants 24 inches apart in full sun and dry, light, well-drained soil. Water sparingly and fertilize little if any. Stake taller plants if needed.

Lantana *(Lantana)*

There are 2 different species of lantana for the garden. Both have gray-green leaves and dense, rounded clusters of tiny flowers. The flowers of *L. Camara* (commonly called Yellow Sage or Red Sage), pictured here, change color as they age. One cluster may have flowers of pink, yellow, and orange at the same time. An upright-growing, shrubby plant, Yellow Sage can reach 2–4 feet in height. *L. montevidensis,* Weeping Lantana, has trailing stems and grows 1 foot high. Its flowers are lilac-pink.

GROWING TIPS

For best results with lantana, buy plants that have been propagated from cuttings or seeds. You can start your own plants from seeds, but it will be 18 weeks before they are ready to go outside. After frost danger has passed and the weather is reliably warm, set lantana plants 12–15 inches apart in full sun and any well-drained soil. Water them lightly and fertilize regularly. Both lantanas can be pruned and trained in numerous ways. In late summer, take and root cuttings and grow them indoors over the winter.

Sweet Pea (*Lathyrus odoratus*)

Hardy

Modern varieties of Sweet Pea have larger flowers and are more heat tolerant than varieties of the past. There are 2 types of Sweet Peas: vines, which climb to 6 feet, and bushy plants, which grow 1½–2½ feet tall. The bushy variety 'Mammoth Mixed' is pictured. Both have highly fragrant, 2-inch flowers in colors of purple, rose, red, white, pink, and blue. Some blooms are solid colored; others are 2-toned. Use the climbing varieties to cover a trellis or fence.

GROWING TIPS

You can start Sweet Pea seeds indoors, but the plants don't like to be transplanted. For better results, sow seeds outdoors in early spring as soon as the soil can be worked; where winters are mild, sow seeds in fall. Clip or nick the seeds before sowing. Plant bushy Sweet Peas 12–15 inches apart and vining types 6–8 inches apart. Give Sweet Peas full sun and deep, rich soil that is well drained and slightly alkaline. Feed plants monthly; water heavily; and mulch the soil to keep it cool and damp.

Lavatera *(Lavatera trimestris)* Hardy

The blooms of Lavatera resemble those of the genus *Malva*. They are cuplike, measuring 2½–4 inches across, flowering in shades of white, pink, or red. The dark green, maplelike foliage often turns bronze in cool weather. The plants have hairy stems that grow 2–3 feet tall.

GROWING TIPS

Lavatera seeds can be started indoors 6–8 weeks before planting time, but they will be difficult to transplant. You will have better luck if you sow seeds outdoors where they are to grow. They are somewhat frost tolerant, so place seeds or plants in the garden in mid-spring. In mild areas, sow seeds in fall for blooms the following spring. Set Lavatera plants 15–18 inches apart in full sun and average to moderately rich, well-drained soil. Feed monthly during the growing and blooming period. Lavatera likes dry soil and does best where nights are cool. To prolong flowering, pick faded flowers.

Meadow Foam (*Limnanthes Douglasii*)

Hardy

M eadow Foam, or Marsh Flower, has pretty, pert, fragrant flowers of yellow, pink, or white, or yellow with white tips. The 5-petaled blooms, each 1 inch across, are borne in such large numbers that they seem to smother the 4- to 12-inch plants, which are clothed in fine, deeply cut leaves.

GROWING TIPS

Meadow Foam plants are usually not available, because they do not transplant well. To grow Meadow Foam, sow seeds outdoors in early spring as soon as the soil can be worked. In mild areas, sow in the fall for bloom the following spring and summer. Select a spot in full sun where the soil is rich, moist, and well drained. After seeds germinate, thin plants to stand 4–6 inches apart. Meadow Foam is native to marsh areas and must be watered heavily. Fertilize at planting time and again when the plant is flowering. Meadow Foam does best in cool climates.

Statice (*Limonium sinuatum*) Tender

One of the best everlastings, Statice has light, delicate, papery flowers. The tiny, funnel-shaped blooms flower in clusters, with colors ranging from white to yellow to red, blue, and purple. The plants grow 12–30 inches tall; they have stiff stems and long leathery foliage. Statice is usually thought of as a flower for drying, but it also makes an attractive hedge.

GROWING TIPS

For early blooms buy bedding plants or start your own Statice plants in-doors, sowing seeds 8–10 weeks before the outside planting date. After all danger of frost has passed, pick a spot in full sun where soil is sandy, light, and well drained, and space plants 18–24 inches apart. (Seeds may be sown outdoors at this time, but the resulting plants will not be as satisfactory.) Fertilize at planting time; no further feeding is necessary. Statice does best with moderate moisture but it will tolerate drought, heat, and salt spray. Hang the flowers upside down to dry.

Edging Lobelia *(Lobelia Erinus)*

Half-hardy

Few annual ground covers can beat the dramatic impact of bright blue to purple Edging Lobelia. The flowers are only ½ inch across, but they completely cover the plants, which grow 3–6 inches high and 12 inches across. Use this lobelia in edgings, borders, rock gardens, and containers. There are also white and red varieties.

GROWING TIPS

Buy Edging Lobelia plants or start your own plants indoors from seeds 10–12 weeks before the last frost, when they can be moved into the garden. Seeds started outdoors are rarely successful. Space the plants 8–10 inches apart in full sun or partial shade and rich, well-drained soil. Lobelia does best where summers are cool; in warmer areas, grow it in shade. Fertilize at planting time and keep the soil evenly moist all summer. A mulch will help to keep the plant roots cool and moist. If lobelia becomes leggy, cut back to encourage a compact habit and heavy bloom. Flowers fall cleanly and do not need to be removed when they fade.

Sweet Alyssum *(Lobularia maritima)*

Half-hardy

Along walkways, near the front door, or in patio pots, Sweet Alyssum, or Snowdrift, is an excellent choice, especially where its heavy fragrance can be appreciated. Domed clusters of tiny white, rose, lavender, or magenta flowers cover plants that are 4–8 inches tall and spread to 12 inches across. The leaves are thin and narrow, like needles. There are many cultivars; 'Rosie O'Day' is pictured. Sweet Alyssum is one of the most reliable annuals, almost never out of bloom.

GROWING TIPS

You can grow Sweet Alyssum from seeds or bedding plants. Sow seeds into the garden several weeks before the last expected frost, or start them indoors 4–6 weeks before the last frost. Set plants out after frost danger has passed, 10–12 inches apart, in full sun or partial shade. Soil should be average and well drained; be sure to fertilize before planting. Sweet Alyssum prefers moist soil and cool nights but grows well almost anywhere. Flowers fall cleanly as they fade and self-sow easily.

Stock *(Matthiola incana)*

A pretty bedding plant in the formal garden and a marvelous cut flower, Stock (also known as Brompton Stock and Gillyflower) is also well loved for its fragrance, which is especially noticeable at night. Stock, which grows 12–24 inches tall, has stiff spikes of inch-long flowers that may be single or double. Colors range from white to cream to pink, rose, red, blue, and purple. Columnar types of Stock produce 1 blooming spike; multi-branching types have several spikes and are more compact. 'Annua', or Ten-Weeks Stock, is pictured.

GROWING TIPS

Stock seeds can be sown outside in mid-spring or, in mild areas, fall, but better results are obtained by starting with plants. You can grow these yourself indoors, starting them 6–8 weeks before the outside planting date. Plants can go into the garden, spaced 12–15 inches apart, in mid-spring. Give them full sun and light, sandy soil that is moist and fertile. Stock does best in cool weather. The terms "7-week" and "10-week," often part of variety names, represent the amount of time from germination to bloom.

Blazing Star *(Mentzelia Lindleyi)* Hardy

The waxy, golden-yellow flowers of Blazing Star open in the evening and stay open until the following noon. Blazing Star is a good choice for gardens viewed at night. The fragrant blooms have 5 petals and are 1½–3 inches across. Blazing Star, with its deeply divided, fernlike leaves, is decorative in beds and borders. It grows 1–2 feet tall.

GROWING TIPS

Blazing Star is best adapted to dry, cool climates, where the seeds can be sown outdoors in fall to bloom in winter. In other climates, seeds may be sown outdoors in early spring as soon as the soil can be worked. They can be started indoors 4–6 weeks before mid-spring planting, but they do not transplant well. Place Blazing Star plants 8–10 inches apart in full sun and light, average to rich soil with excellent drainage. They like moisture, but will tolerate drought. Feed them at planting time and again 2 months later.

Ice Plant *(Mesembryanthemum crystallinum)*

Tender

Ice Plant got its common name because the leaves are covered with specks that glisten in the sunlight like pieces of ice. It is sometimes called Sea Fig or Sea Marigold because it grows along the coast. The plants grow 8 inches high and 1–2 feet across and have showy, daisy-like, 1¼-inch flowers of white, pink, magenta, or yellow. Ice Plant is a perennial in California, where it is used widely as a ground cover and rock garden plant. In other areas, it can be treated as a tender annual; it does well by the seashore.

GROWING TIPS

It is best to use purchased plants, or sow seeds indoors 10–12 weeks before the last frost, when seedlings can be moved outside. The seeds, which are very fine, need darkness to sprout, so cover flats with black plastic until seeds germinate. Space plants 8–12 inches apart, in full sun and dry, poor soil that is well drained. Fertilize them at planting time; if you are growing them as perennials, feed them again in 2 months. Ice Plant blooms best before summer becomes hot and will stay in bloom for 4–6 weeks.

Monkey Flower *(Mimulus)*

Half-hardy

The showy, 2-lipped flowers of M. *guttatus* and its hybrids, M. × *hybridus* (pictured), look something like little faces. The tubular, 1- to 2-inch blooms are yellow, gold, or red, and sometimes flecked with a contrasting color. The foliage is often sticky. Monkey Flowers, which grow 6–12 inches high, are used in beds, borders, and hanging baskets, and do well near water.

GROWING TIPS

Monkey Flower can be started from cuttings or purchased plants, or from seeds started indoors 6–8 weeks before outside planting time. If you start your own seeds, you will need fluorescent lights, because the seedlings need 13 hours of light to grow. Plant Monkey Flowers outdoors in early spring to mid-spring, 6 inches apart, in rich, moist, well-drained soil. Feed them at planting time and apply a mulch to keep the soil cool and moist. Monkey Flowers do best in partial to full shade, but will grow in full sun if it is cool. They prefer cool and humid summers; in hot areas, they seem almost to dissolve.

Forget-Me-Not (*Myosotis sylvatica*) Hardy

There is a Forget-Me-Not that is a perennial, but this species is a true annual. It grows 6–8 inches high and spreads to 10 inches across, making it a good ground cover to contrast with spring bulbs and early perennials. The flowers are tiny, up to ½ inch across, and usually blue with a yellow center, although there also are pink and white varieties.

GROWING TIPS

Forget-Me-Not will bloom when weather is cool. If seeds are sown outdoors in fall, plants will bloom the following spring. If sown in early spring, they may not bloom until fall, but will follow a spring-blooming schedule after that, as they self-sow readily. Seeds can be sown indoors, but with difficulty, as they germinate at 55° F. Space your Forget-Me-Nots 6–8 inches apart in very rich, moist or wet soil that is well drained. They grow best in light shade in a cool spot. Fertilize them at planting time and again every spring if you allow Forget-Me-Not to self-sow.

Baby Blue-Eyes *(Nemophila Menziesii)*   Hardy

Baby Blue-Eyes are low, trailing plants with fragrant bell-shaped flowers. They have hairy, 12-inch-long stems covered with decorative, deeply cut leaves. The flowers, which are 1½ inches across, bloom at the tips of the branches. They are solid blue, solid white, or bright blue with white centers. Baby Blue-Eyes is best used in rock gardens or naturalistic gardens, or as a ground cover.

GROWING TIPS

Baby Blue-Eyes is a cool-weather plant. Sow seeds outdoors in early spring as soon as the soil can be worked. In mild climates, sow seeds in the fall for bloom the following spring. Seeds can be started indoors if a temperature of 55° F can be maintained. Space plants 8–12 inches apart in light shade and light, sandy, well-drained soil. Baby Blue-Eyes self-sows easily. Fertilize at planting time and again every spring if new plants volunteer. If possible, shelter Baby Blue-Eyes from the wind.

Flowering Tobacco *(Nicotiana alata)*   Tender

A relative of commercially grown tobacco, Flowering Tobacco has 2-inch-long, trumpet-shaped blooms. It usually grows 10–18 inches tall and is covered with fuzzy, slightly sticky leaves. The flowers bloom all summer in loose, upright bunches. They may be yellow, purple, white, green, pink, or red. The flowers of modern hybrids stay open all day, although they have lost most of the sweet aroma that was once associated with Flowering Tobacco.

GROWING TIPS

Flowering Tobacco seeds can be sown outdoors after all danger of frost has passed; for earlier bloom, start with purchased plants, or start seeds indoors 6–8 weeks earlier. Space the plants 10–12 inches apart in full sun or partial shade and rich, well-drained soil. Where summers are hot, keep the plants well watered; they like high humidity. Feed Flowering Tobacco at planting time. Cut off dead flower stalks to keep the plants blooming all summer. They may self-sow.

Cupflower

(Nierembergia hippomanica var. *violacea)* Half-hardy

The blooms of this annual, as the name suggests, are shaped like cups. The 1-inch flowers cover the mounded, 6- to 15-inch plants. Most varieties are blue or blue-violet with a yellow center ('Purple Robe' is pictured), although there are also white varieties. The leaves are hairy and finely divided. Cupflowers are best used as border, edging, or rock garden plants, or in hanging containers.

GROWING TIPS

Begin with purchased plants, or start your own plants indoors 10–12 weeks before planting time. Plants are slightly frost tolerant and can be planted 2–3 weeks before the last frost. Space them 6–9 inches apart in full sun to light shade and light, moist, well-drained soil. Fertilize when you plant them and again every other month. Cupflower grows best in warm weather.

Love-in-a-Mist *(Nigella damascena)*

Hardy

The flowers of Love-in-a-Mist sit within collars of fine, thready, delicate leaves that give the impression of mist (although not everyone thinks so—this plant is also called Devil-in-the-Bush). Blooms are pink, red, blue, white, or purple, with tapered petals and prominent stamens. Love-in-a-Mist plants grow 1–2 feet high. After they flower, nutmeg-scented seeds form in round, green seedpods with red markings. Love-in-a-Mist is a good plant for borders. The blooms, which are pretty cut flowers, can also be dried.

GROWING TIPS

Start sowing Love-in-a-Mist seeds outdoors in early spring and resow every 2 weeks until early summer, as they have a short blooming period. In mild climates, sow seeds in fall. Seeds can be started indoors but the seedlings don't like to be transplanted. Space the plants 8–10 inches apart, in full sun and average, moist garden soil with excellent drainage. Feed the plants monthly when they are blooming. Love-in-a-Mist prefers cool weather and self-sows easily if the seedpods are left on the plants.

Evening Primrose *(Oenothera)* Hardy

These *Oenothera* plants are called evening primroses because some of them open only in the evening. There are, however, species that bloom during the day, which are sometimes called sundrops. All have showy, single flowers with 4 petals or lobes. Missouri Evening Primrose, *O. missourensis* (shown here), is night-blooming, with 5-inch yellow flowers on 15-inch plants. Showy Evening Primrose, *O. speciosa,* has 3-inch white flowers that bloom in the daytime on 1- to 2-foot plants. Both are perennials that can be grown as annuals.

GROWING TIPS

To grow evening primroses as annuals, sow seeds outdoors in early spring; in mild climates, you can sow them in fall. Seeds can also be started indoors 8–12 weeks before planting time, or plants can be propagated by division. Set plants into the garden in early spring, spacing them 6–8 inches apart. Evening primroses grow equally well in full sun or partial shade and are not fussy about soil, as long as it is well drained. They need no fertilizing but should be watered when the ground is dry.

Poppy *(Papaver)*

The petals of poppies look as if they are made of crepe paper. Flowers, which may be single or double, are 1–3 inches across. Their stems are wiry, standing above deeply cut leaves. Some poppies are perennials but others are annuals. Iceland Poppy, *P. nudicaule* (pictured), grows 1 foot high and has blooms of white, pink, yellow, orange, or red. Corn Poppy, *P. Rhoeas* (also known as Flanders Poppy or Shirley Poppy), reaches a height of 3 feet and has flowers of red, purple, or white. Use poppies as accent plants and in mixed beds.

GROWING TIPS

You can start poppy seeds indoors if you have a room that is 55° F, but the plants do not like to be moved. A better alternative is to sow the seeds outdoors in late fall or early spring. Thin the seedlings to 8–12 inches apart. Give them full sun and rich, dry soil with excellent drainage. Be very careful not to overwater. Fertilize at planting time but do not feed the plants again. Poppies grow best during cool weather. For continual blooming of Corn Poppies, sow seeds every 2 weeks in spring and summer.

Martha Washington Geranium
(Pelargonium × domesticum)

Tender

Martha Washington Geranium is sometimes called Lady Washington Geranium, Regal Geranium, or Summer Azalea. The showy flowers, which may be white, pink, or red, have dark blotches on the upper petals. Blooms measure 1½–3 inches across and grow on 12- to 18-inch plants. Leaves are toothed and deeply lobed. Martha Washingtons will bloom over a long period in beds, borders, or containers, as long as nights are cool.

GROWING TIPS
Martha Washington Geraniums cannot be grown from seeds. Buy plants or root stem cuttings from existing plants. Place them outdoors after the last frost, spaced 8–10 inches apart. Martha Washingtons prefer partial shade and very rich, slightly acid, well-drained soil. Keep them well watered but, if possible, keep the leaves dry to prevent disease. Fertilize at planting time and again each month. Pick faded flowers to prolong the bloom. Mulch to keep the soil moist and cool.

Zonal Geranium *(Pelargonium × hortorum)* Tender

For beds, borders, and containers, Zonal (or Fish) Geranium is one of the most popular annual garden plants. Rounded flower heads bloom from mid-spring until frost over heart-shaped, scalloped, sometimes banded foliage. The blooms, which measure up to 5 inches across, may be white, pink, red, orange, or lavender. The plants reach 1–3 feet.

GROWING TIPS
Depending on the variety, Zonal Geraniums are propagated from seeds or by cuttings. To start your own plants from seeds, you must give them a 12- to 16-week head start indoors. If you buy plants, look for varieties grown from cuttings if you plan to use containers and varieties grown from seeds for massed plantings. The seed-grown varieties are more tolerant of heat, high humidity, and disease. Plant both types in full sun after the last frost in ordinary, well-drained soil. Water the plants well, fertilize monthly, and remove faded blooms. Take cuttings to start next year's plants.

Common Garden Petunia
(Petunia × hybrida)

Half-hardy

Petunias have been among the most popular garden annuals for years, and for good reason. Spreading or cascading over beds or baskets, they have trumpet-shaped, single or double flowers in every color of the rainbow. Many are solid colored; others are starred, zoned, splashed, speckled, striped, veined, or edged with a contrasting color. Choose grandiflora petunias, with 5-inch-wide flowers, for containers ('Flash Series' is pictured); and multifloras, with large numbers of 2- to 3-inch flowers, for massed beds. Petunias range from 8–18 inches high.

GROWING TIPS

Buy petunia plants or start your own indoors by sowing seeds 10–12 weeks before the last frost, when the plants can be moved into the garden. Space them 8–12 inches apart, in full sun or light shade. Petunias grow well in dry or sandy soil; if your soil is heavy, poor, or alkaline, use the single-flowered varieties rather than the double. Petunias like high temperatures and tolerate heat and drought well. Pinch them at planting time to make them bushier; if they become leggy, cut them back.

Annual Phlox *(Phlox Drummondii)*

Hardy

Unlike the tall perennial phloxes, Annual Phlox, or Drummond Phlox, is compact and low-growing. The plants are mounded, 6–18 inches high, and are covered with long, thin leaves and topped by round or star-shaped flowers. Individual flowers are only about 1 inch across, but they appear in clusters. Colors include white, pink, red, blue, lavender, purple, yellow, and salmon. Use Annual Phlox for edges, borders, rock gardens, and containers.

GROWING TIPS

Annual Phlox can tolerate a little frost, so plants or seeds can go into the garden as soon as the soil can be worked in early spring. You can start seeds indoors, but they need to be grown in individual pots at 55° F for 10 weeks before transplanting and they don't like being moved. Space plants 6 inches apart in full sun; they do best in rich, light, sandy soil with good drainage. Feed Annual Phlox monthly and keep it well watered. It may decline somewhat in midsummer heat.

Creamcups *(Platystemon californicus)* Hardy

Creamcups are branching plants covered with delicate, thready leaves. They grow 6–12 inches high. The flowers, which are 1 inch across, have 6 petals and are light yellow or cream colored. In the center of each flower are tufts of numerous, petal-like stamens. Creamcups can be used in the rock garden, as a ground cover, or as a low edging plant.

GROWING TIPS

Sow Creamcups seeds outdoors in early spring as soon as the ground can be worked. Thin the plants to stand 10–12 inches apart. Creamcups like full sun and sandy, well-drained soil, which should be heavily watered but not soggy. Add fertilizer to the soil before planting; no further feeding is necessary.

Portulaca *(Portulaca grandiflora)*

Tender

Portulaca, or Rose Moss, is a much-branched, ground-hugging plant that is perfect for dry slopes, beds, and rock gardens. A succulent plant growing only 4–6 inches high, it has soft, fleshy, often reddish stems and thick, needle-like, often spoon-shaped leaves. The flowers, which are 1–2 inches across, are ruffled. Some varieties are single, flat, and cup shaped; others are double, resembling tiny roses. Flowers may be white, cream, pink, red, yellow, gold, orange, or salmon. They open only in full sun.

GROWING TIPS

Set Portulaca seeds or plants into the garden after all danger of frost has passed, or start seeds indoors 8–10 weeks earlier. Space the plants 12–15 inches apart in full sun and dry, sandy, well-drained soil. Little if any fertilizing is needed. Portulaca is very tolerant of heat and drought and should be watered very sparingly. Flowers fall cleanly from the plant, and seeds resow easily each year.

German Primrose *(Primula obconica)*

Hardy

The flower clusters of German Primrose may be purple, pink, red, or white. The individual flowers are single, measuring 1 inch across. The cluster blooms on a 12-inch, leafless stem over heart-shaped, frilled leaves. Like all primroses, German Primrose prefers cool weather and blooms best in the spring or early summer.

GROWING TIPS

It takes a long time to grow German Primrose from seeds, so it is easier to buy plants and to set them into the garden in early spring. If you want to start your own plants from seeds, sow them 6 months in advance, after first chilling the seeds in the refrigerator for 3 weeks. Seeds can also be sown in the garden in late fall. Space German Primrose plants 8–10 inches apart, in partial shade; they prefer a rich, slightly acid, well-drained soil. Keep the plants well watered and mulch them to keep the soil cool and moist. Fertilize German Primroses while they are growing or blooming. They can cause a skin rash; wear gloves when you handle them.

Gloriosa Daisy (*Rudbeckia hirta*)

Half-hardy

Gloriosa Daisies are related to the Black-eyed Susans that often bloom along roadsides. Gloriosa Daisies have golden, yellow, bronze, orange, or brown flowers with dark brown or black centers. The 3- to 6-inch, single or double blooms appear all summer until frost. The plants grow 8–36 inches tall in an upright, branching habit. Gloriosa Daisies can be used in beds or borders, but also fit well into the naturalistic or wildflower garden. They are a good flower for cutting.

GROWING TIPS

You can plant Gloriosa Daisy seeds in the garden after frost danger has passed, but for early bloom, start with plants. If you grow your own plants, start the seeds indoors 6–8 weeks before transplanting time. Space plants 12–24 inches apart, in full sun or light shade. Gloriosa Daisies prefer rich, moist soil, but will grow well where soil is poor and dry. They are also very heat tolerant. Incorporate fertilizer at planting time, but do not feed them again. Cut off old flowers as they fade; they self-sow easily.

Painted-Tongue *(Salpiglossis sinuata)*

The velvety flowers of Painted-Tongue are blue, purple, yellow, pink, or red, and often are "painted" or veined in a contrasting color. Each trumpet-shaped flower is 2–2½ inches across. The plants grow 2–3 feet tall and have hairy leaves and stems. Painted-Tongue is used in beds and borders. In areas where it is too cool to grow petunias well, Painted-Tongue makes a good substitute.

GROWING TIPS

Sow Painted-Tongue seeds into the garden in mid-spring, several weeks before the last expected frost. For earlier bloom and a better chance of success, buy plants or start your own indoors 8 weeks before planting time. Seeds need darkness to sprout, so cover flats with black plastic until they germinate. Set plants out in mid-spring, spaced 8–12 inches apart; they grow best in rich, well-drained, alkaline soil. Fertilize once when planting. Water and mulch heavily to keep the soil moist and cool.

Sage (*Salvia*)

Two sages are popular for the annual flower garden, in beds, massed plantings, borders, or as cut flowers. Mealy-Cup Sage, *S. farinacea* (the variety 'Victoria' is shown here), has rich violet-blue, medium blue, or white flowers blooming in thin spikes all summer. The plants are 18–24 inches tall; foliage is a contrasting gray-green. *S. splendens,* sometimes called Scarlet Sage, has pyramidal spikes of flowers, primarily red, but also white, blue, purple, or salmon. They bloom over dark green, waxy leaves. The plants grow from 6–24 inches tall.

GROWING TIPS

Salvia seeds cannot be started successfully outdoors, so buy plants or grow your own, starting them inside 8–10 weeks before the last frost for *S. splendens,* and 12 weeks before for *S. farinacea.* Salvias grow much better if they are not in bloom when they are planted. Set them out after the last frost, spacing them 6–12 inches apart, depending on their mature size, in full sun or partial shade. They grow best in rich, well-drained soil that is kept moist, though they will also tolerate dry soil. Feed salvias lightly if at all.

Scabious (*Scabiosa*)

There are 2 species of scabious grown in the annual garden, and they are completely different in appearance and use. *S. atropurpurea,* Pincushion Flower or Sweet Scabious (pictured), has fragrant double flowers that may be blue, pink, purple, white, or red. Silvery filaments protrude from the 2- to 4-inch blooms. Pincushion Flower, which grows 1½–3 feet tall, is used in borders and for cut flowers. Starflower, *S. stellata,* has 1¼-inch, blue or rose-violet, star-shaped flowers. Starflower plants grow to 2 feet tall.

GROWING TIPS

For best results with either *Scabiosa* species, begin with purchased plants or plants you started indoors 4–5 weeks before planting time. Plant both species after the last frost. Place them in full sun, spaced 10–15 inches apart. They will grow in average soil but will do best in soil that is rich, alkaline, and well-drained. Fertilize them at planting time and again every month. Water when the soil is dry. If possible, water in the morning; foliage that is wet all night is prone to disease. Tall varieties may need to be staked.

Dusty Miller *(Senecio Cineraria)*

Half-hardy

Dusty Miller is a common name given to a group of plants with silver or gray foliage. *S. Cineraria* is one of the most common of these, although there are other species and even different genera that are almost identical in appearance and care. All are grown for their foliage and are used as edgings, buffers between strong colors, or in gardens that are viewed at night. The plants grow up to 30 inches high and have lobed to finely cut leaves. The variety 'Silver Dust' is shown here.

GROWING TIPS

Dusty Miller seeds cannot be started outdoors, so buy plants or start your own indoors 8–10 weeks before moving them outside after the last frost. Space the plants 10–12 inches apart, in full sun or light shade and light, sandy, well-drained soil. Water lightly, allowing the soil to dry out between waterings. Incorporate fertilizer into the soil before planting; no further feeding is necessary. Dusty Miller can be cut back if it becomes leggy.

African Marigold *(Tagetes erecta)*

Half-hardy

Traditionally, African (or Aztec) Marigolds were 3-foot-tall plants topped by very full, double or carnationlike flowers up to 5 inches across. Newer hybrids are more compact, growing 1–2 feet high, but still bear the large flowers. The blooms are in the yellow, gold, and orange ranges. The foliage is highly scented and deeply cut.

GROWING TIPS

African Marigold seeds will germinate and grow outdoors, but they will not bloom until late summer, because the plants are sensitive to day length. To ensure summer-long bloom, buy plants or start your own indoors 4–6 weeks before the last frost and make sure they are in bud or bloom when you plant them. Plant African Marigolds in full sun and average, well-drained soil. Water whenever the soil is dry. Space African Marigold plants a distance apart equal to half their mature height. Fertilize them monthly and pick off flowers as they fade to ensure continuous bloom. Newer African Marigold hybrids do not need to be staked.

French Marigold *(Tagetes patula)*

Half-hardy

Growing 6–18 inches tall, French Marigolds are shorter and more compact than African Marigolds. The flowers, which range from 1–2½ inches across, may be single or double, or may have a central crest. They are yellow, gold, orange, mahogany, or deep red. 'Queen Sophia', a double form, is shown here. The foliage is scented and deeply cut. Crosses between French and African marigolds are called triploids or "mules" and are similar in appearance to French Marigolds. The scent of marigolds is said to repel nematodes.

GROWING TIPS

French Marigold seeds can be started outdoors, or indoors 4–6 weeks before plants are to go outside. Triploid marigolds should be started indoors. Once frost danger has passed, plant marigolds, spacing them 4–8 inches apart. Give them a spot in full sun with average, well-drained soil. Remove the flowers of French Marigolds as soon as they fade; you do not have to remove the faded flowers of triploids, because they do not set seed. Water marigolds when the ground is dry and fertilize them monthly.

Mexican Sunflower *(Tithonia rotundifolia)* Tender

exican Sunflowers have 3-inch, daisylike flowers of orange-red or yellow that bloom from mid-summer until frost. The plants are tall and shrubby, growing 3–6 feet high. The foliage can grow to 12 inches in length and is gray and velvety. Mexican Sunflower is brilliant in the garden as a backdrop to other plants or as a hedge. It is also widely used in cutting gardens.

GROWING TIPS

It is easiest to grow Mexican Sunflower from plants. Either buy them or start your own indoors 6–8 weeks before the last frost, when they can be moved outdoors. Choose a place in full sun with average garden soil and good drainage. Space the plants 2–3 feet apart. Mexican Sunflower is very tolerant of heat and drought and should not be over-watered. Feed it lightly each month. Cut buds when they are still tight for long-lasting cut flowers.

Wishbone Flower *(Torenia Fournieri)*

Tender

Wishbone Flowers are compact, neat, mounded plants, growing 8–12 inches high. Flowers cover the plant, nearly hiding the pointed leaves. The ¾-inch blooms have a light violet or pale blue upper lip, a purple lower lip, and a yellow or white throat. In the throat is a pair of stamens that looks like a wishbone. From a distance, Wishbone Flower looks like a pansy, but is much different upon closer examination. Use Wishbone Flower as an edging or border plant or in massed plantings or planters.

Growing Tips

Wishbone Flower cannot be grown from seeds sown outdoors. Buy plants, or start them indoors 10–12 weeks before the last frost, when they can be moved outside. Space the plants 6–8 inches apart. They prefer partial or full shade, but they will grow in sun where night temperatures fall below 65° F. When shaded, Wishbone Flower is quite heat tolerant. It grows best in soil that is fertile, moist, and well drained.

Blue Laceflower *(Trachymene coerulea)* Hardy

Imagine Queen Anne's Lace colored light blue and you have the blooms of Blue Laceflower. Tiny sweetly scented flowers bloom in 2- to 3-inch flat-topped clusters. Stems grow 1½–2½ feet tall over lacy foliage. Blue Laceflower is used in the middle of mixed borders or in the cutting garden.

GROWING TIPS
Young Blue Laceflower plants have a long taproot and do not like to be transplanted, so if you start seeds indoors, sow them in individual pots. It is better if you sow seeds outdoors in spring several weeks before the last expected frost. Thin the plants to 8–10 inches apart; keeping them somewhat crowded improves bloom and eliminates the need for staking. Grow them in full sun; they do best in a rich, sandy soil that is well drained. Blue Laceflower prefers cool weather; apply a mulch in hot areas to keep the soil cool and water often to keep the ground moist.

Nasturtium *(Tropaeolum majus)*   Tender

Nasturtiums are rapid-growing annuals that occur in 2 forms. They are either bushy, growing 12–18 inches tall, or trailing, with stems that can reach 8 feet in length. The flowers of both types are 2–2½ inches across and may be either single or double. Some are fragrant. Blooms are red, pink, mahogany, yellow, or orange, and sometimes spotted. The dull, round leaves are 2–7 inches across. Depending on the type, Nasturtiums can be used as bedding plants, in hanging baskets, or on trellises.

GROWING TIPS

Nasturtium seeds germinate and grow quickly, but the seedlings do not like to be transplanted, so it is best to sow seeds directly into the garden. Sow them after frost danger has passed; thin the young plants to 8–12 inches apart. Select a place with full sun or light shade and poor, light soil that is well drained. Rich soil gives you abundant foliage but few flowers. Do not fertilize Nasturtiums; water only when the soil is dry. They prefer a cool, humid climate. In warm areas, the bushy types grow better.

Garden Verbena *(Verbena × hybrida)* Tender

Garden Verbena plants make a stunning show of color. The flowers, which bloom in clusters 2½–4 inches across, are white, red, violet, purple, blue, cream, rose, or pink; 'Pink Bouquet' is shown here. Many of the flowers have a contrasting white eye. Depending on the variety, verbena hybrids may be either upright or spreading, growing 8–12 inches high. The foliage is deeply quilted or textured. Use Garden Verbena as edging, bedding, ground cover, rock garden, or container plants.

GROWING TIPS
You will have most success growing Garden Verbena from purchased plants. The seeds cannot be sown outdoors; seeds sown indoors need 10–12 weeks' growth before the last frost and usually only half of those sown will germinate. Plant Garden Verbena in full sun, spacing the upright types 8 inches apart and the spreading types 12 inches apart. Verbena prefers a light, rich, well-drained soil, but it will tolerate poor soil. Fertilize Garden Verbena monthly. It is very tolerant of heat and drought.

Pansy *(Viola × Wittrockiana)*

Many pansies seem to have faces on their petals; others are 2-toned or solid-colored. Blooms may be yellow, purple, blue, red, white, pink, bronze, lavender, or orange. Pansies are often classified in two groups. The multifloras have large numbers of 2- to 2½-inch flowers ('Clear Crystal Mix' is shown here); the grandifloras have 4-inch flowers. Pansy plants grow 6–9 inches high. Although pansy is an early spring plant, heat-resistant varieties will bloom into summer.

GROWING TIPS

Add pansy plants to the garden in early spring as soon as the soil can be worked. Where winter temperatures do not drop below 20° F, pansies can be planted in the fall and mulched over winter for bloom early the following spring. Pansy seeds do not do well outside but can be started indoors 14 weeks before planting. Pansies prefer full sun and moist, fertile soil. Mulch the soil to keep the roots cool and damp. Pick flowers as soon as they fade to extend the blooming period.

Common Zinnia *(Zinnia elegans)*

It seems a shame that one of the finest annuals for the garden is always at the end of the list. Zinnias, which have single or double flowers ranging from the size of buttons to several inches across, bloom in every color except blue. The smallest zinnias grow only 6 inches high; the tallest varieties reach 4 feet. Depending on the size, use zinnias for edgings, borders, mixed beds, backgrounds, containers, or cut flowers.

GROWING TIPS

Zinnias grow easily and quickly from seed, which may be sown outside as soon as frost danger has passed. You may also start seeds indoors 4 weeks earlier, or purchase zinnia plants. Set zinnias out in full sun, 6–24 inches apart, depending on their ultimate size, in fertile, well-drained soil. Do not crowd the plants—air circulation will inhibit mildew disease. Pinch zinnias when they are first planted to make them bushy. Cut flowers as soon as they fade to encourage further bloom.

APPENDICES

FROST DATE MAP

Legend specifies approximate date
of last spring frost and number of
days in growing season.

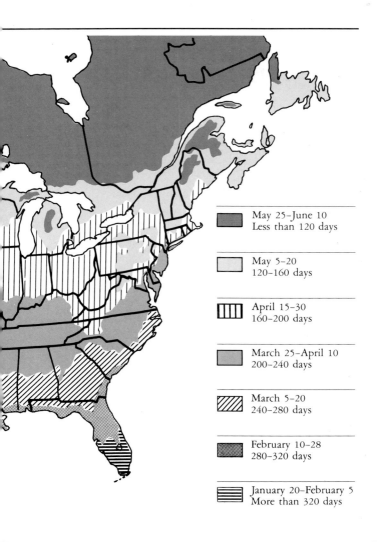

May 25–June 10
Less than 120 days

May 5–20
120–160 days

April 15–30
160–200 days

March 25–April 10
200–240 days

March 5–20
240–280 days

February 10–28
280–320 days

January 20–February 5
More than 320 days

GARDEN PESTS AND DISEASES

PLANT PESTS and diseases are a fact of life for a gardener. Therefore, it is helpful to become familiar with common pests and diseases in your area and to learn how to control them.

Symptoms of Plant Problems

Because the same general symptoms are associated with many diseases and pests, some experience is needed to determine their causes.

Diseases

Both fungi and bacteria are responsible for a variety of diseases ranging from leaf spots and wilts to root rot, but bacterial diseases usually make the affected plant tissues appear wetter than fungi do. Diseases caused by viruses and mycoplasma, often transmitted by aphids and leafhoppers, display such symptoms as mottled yellow or deformed leaves and twisted or stunted growth. Aster yellows, one such mycoplasma disease, affects marigolds, asters, and some other annuals.

Insect Pests

Numerous insects attack plants. Sap-sucking insects—including aphids, leafhoppers, and scale insects—suck plant juices. The affected plant becomes yellow, stunted, and misshapen. Aphids and scale insects produce honeydew, a sticky substance that attracts ants and sooty mold fungus growth. Other pests with rasping-sucking mouthparts, such as thrips and spider mites, scrape plant tissue and then suck the juices that well up in the injured areas.

Leaf-chewers, namely beetles and caterpillars, consume plant leaves, whole or in part. Leaf miners make tunnels within the leaves, creating brown trails and causing leaf tissue to dry. In contrast, borers tunnel into shoots and stems, and their young larvae consume plant tissue, weakening the plant. Some insects, such as various grubs and maggots, feed on roots, weakening or killing the plant.

Nematodes

Microscopic roundworms called nematodes are other pests that attack roots and cause stunting and poor plant growth. Some kinds of nematodes produce galls on roots, while others produce them on leaves.

Environmental Stresses

Some types of plant illness result from environment-related stress, such as severe wind, drought, flooding, or extreme cold. Other problems are caused by salt toxicity, rodents, birds, nutritional deficiencies or excesses, pesticides, or damage from lawn mowers. Many of these injuries are avoidable if you take proper precautions.

Controlling Plant Problems

Always buy healthy disease- and insect-free plants, and select resistant varieties when available. Check leaves and stems for dead areas or off-color and stunted tissue. Later, when you plant your flowers, be sure to prepare the soil properly.

Routine Preventives

By cultivating the soil routinely you will expose insects and disease-causing organisms to the sun and thus lessen their chances of surviving in your garden. In the fall, be sure to destroy infested or diseased plants, remove dead leaves and flowers, and clean up plant debris. Do not add diseased or infested material to the compost pile. Spray plants with water from time to time to dislodge insect pests and remove suffocating dust. Pick off the larger insects by hand. To discourage fungal leaf spots and blights, always water plants in the morning and allow the leaves to dry off before nightfall. For the same reason, provide adequate air circulation around leaves and stems by spacing plants properly.

Weeds provide a home for insects and diseases, so pull them up or use pre-emergent herbicides. We do not recommend the use of any other type in the annual garden. If you use herbicides on your lawn, do not spray them near your annuals or apply them on a windy day.

Insecticides and Fungicides

To protect plant tissue from injury due to insects and diseases, a number of insecticides and fungicides are available. However, few products control diseases due to bacteria, viruses, and mycoplasma. Pesticides are usually either "protectant" or "systemic" in nature. Protectants keep insects or disease organisms away from uninfected foliage, while systemics move through the plant and provide some therapeutic or eradicant action as well as protection. Botanical insecticides such as pyrethrum and rotenone have a shorter residual effect on pests but are considered less toxic and generally safer for the user and the environment than inorganic chemical insecticides. Biological control through the use of organisms like *Bacillus thuringiensis* (a bacterium toxic to moth and butterfly larvae) is effective and safe.

Recommended pesticides may vary to some extent from region to region. Consult your local Cooperative Extension Service or plant professional regarding the appropriate material to use. Always check the pesticide label to be sure that it is registered for use on the pest and plant with which you are dealing. Follow the label concerning safety precautions, dosage, and frequency of application.

AN ANNUAL
CUTTING GARDEN

A CUTTING garden can double your enjoyment of your annual plants: It is attractive in itself, and the cut flowers you reap from it will bring its beauty and scent into your home.

Starting a Cutting Garden

An easy way to begin planning your cutting garden is to look through seed catalogs, noting the shapes and colors of different annuals. Many companies offer packets of assorted seeds of plants suitable for cutting. These packets are full of surprises: you won't know what flowers you have until they come up. If you wish to plan your cutting garden more carefully, keep a few guidelines in mind. Decide how much space you can devote to a cutting garden and estimate the number of plants your space will accommodate. When you make this estimate, consider planting successive crops to make the most of your space and count these plants as well. When you choose plants, include the three basic flower forms: spire-shaped flowers, which add height and line to arrangements; round flowers for mass; and lacy, delicate flowers, which serve as a filler without adding mass. Choose colors and tones that are compatible. You might also include some foliage plants.

How to Cut Flowers

The best time to cut flowers is when it is cool; either in the morning after the dew has dried or just before sundown. Do not cut them during midday heat. Cut the stems diagonally with a knife; do not use scissors, because they can crush the stems. Place the flowers in water immediately and keep them out of direct sunlight, until you are ready to arrange them. To revive wilted flowers, stand them in warm water.

Arranging Cut Flowers

Before starting your arrangement, strip off all leaves that will be underwater. Select an appropriate container; a loose arrangement of field flowers might look fine in a mason jar, while a more formal arrangement may call for a crystal vase. The size of the container should be in proportion to the height of the arrangement. A good rule of thumb is to make the arrangement two and a half times the height of the container.

Principles of Design

Flower arrangements are made up of lines, masses, and spaces. Lines can be manipulated to produce a sense of depth. Mass is dependent not only on the size of flowers, but on their color and texture. The spaces between flowers accentuate the line and mass of a composition.

Most arrangements fall into four basic categories: vertical, horizontal, circular, and triangular. The form you choose will depend upon the flowers, the container, and the space the arrangement will occupy. Vertical arrangements work well against a bare wall. Horizontal and circular compositions look good on low tables and as informal centerpieces. Triangular designs can be adapted to almost any setting.

Texture and Color

Manipulation of textures is an important principle of flower arranging. Some textures convey weight, while others look airy. Shiny textures reflect light and therefore add brightness. Rough, fluffy, and prickly surfaces bring informality to a design. Try experimenting with different textures to achieve a balance in your composition.

Color is best used discreetly. A monochromatic arrangement with both dark and light values of a single color can be very effective, as can a design using closely related hues, such as reds and oranges or blues and purples. For a more dramatic effect, use complementary colors (you can pick up a color wheel at an art-supply store to learn more about color). Blue and orange is a striking combination; purple and yellow and red and green are also complementary.

Preserving Cut Flowers

Keep your flowers looking fresh by changing the water and recutting the stems every day or so. If you are planning an arrangement for a party, cut the flowers several days ahead, before the buds fully open, and refrigerate them in water until you need them. Put them into fresh water after you bring them out.

GLOSSARY

Acid soil
Soil with a pH value lower than 7.

Alkaline soil
Soil with a pH value of more than 7.

Annual
A plant whose entire life span, from sprouting to flowering and producing seeds, is encompassed in a single growing season.

Axil
The angle between a leafstalk and the stem from which it grows.

Basal leaf
A leaf at the base of a stem.

Biennial
A plant whose life span extends to two growing seasons, sprouting in the first growing season and then flowering, producing seed, and dying in the second.

Blade
The broad, flat part of a leaf.

Bract
A modified and often scalelike leaf, usually located at the base of a flower, a fruit, or a cluster of flowers or fruits.

Bud
A young and undeveloped leaf, flower, or shoot, usually covered tightly with scales.

Bulb
A short underground stem, the swollen portion consisting mostly of fleshy, food-storing scale leaves.

Calyx
Collectively, the sepals of a flower.

Clasping
Surrounding or partly surrounding the stem, as in the base of the leaves of certain plants.

Compound leaf
A leaf made up of two or more leaflets.

Corm
A solid underground stem, resembling a bulb but lacking scales; often with a membranous coat.

Corolla
Collectively, the petals of a flower.

Creeping
Prostrate or trailing over the ground or over other plants.

Crest
A ridge or appendage on petals, flower clusters, or leaves.

Cross-pollination
The transfer of pollen from one plant to another.

Crown
That part of a plant between the roots and the stem, usually at soil level.

Cultivar
An unvarying plant variety, maintained by vegetative propagation or by inbred seed.

Cutting
A piece of plant without roots; set in a rooting medium, it develops roots and is then potted as a new plant.

Dead-heading
Removing blooms that are spent.

Deciduous
Dropping its leaves; not evergreen.

Disbudding
The pinching off of selected buds to benefit those left to grow.

Disk flower
The small tubular flowers in the central part of a floral head, as in most members of the daisy family. Also called a disk floret.

Division
Propagation by division of crowns, roots, or tubers into segments that can be induced to send out roots.

Double-flowered
Having more than the usual number of petals, usually arranged in extra rows.

Evergreen
Retaining leaves for most or all of an annual cycle.

Everlasting
A plant whose flowers can be prepared for dried arrangements.

Filament
The threadlike lower portion of a stamen.

Genus
A group of closely related species; plural, genera.

Germinate
To sprout.

Herb
A plant without a permanent, woody stem, usually dying back during cold weather.

Herbaceous perennial
An herb that dies back each fall, but sends out new shoots and flowers for several successive years.

Horticulture
The cultivation of plants for ornament or food.

Humus
Partly or wholly decomposed vegetable matter; an important constituent of garden soil.

Hybird
A plant resulting from a cross between two parent plants belonging to different species, subspecies, or genera.

Invasive
Aggressively spreading away from the site of cultivation.

Leaflet
One of the subdivisions of a compound leaf.

Loam
A humus-rich soil containing up to 25 percent clay, up to 50 percent silt, and less than 50 percent sand.

Lobe
A segment of a cleft leaf or petal.

Margin
The edge of a leaf.

Mulch
A protective covering spread over the soil around the base of plants to retard evaporation, control temperature, or enrich the soil.

Neutral soil
Soil that is neither acid nor alkaline, having a pH value of 7.

Node
The place on the stem where leaves or branches are attached.

Peat moss
Partly decomposed moss, rich in nutrients and with a high water retention, used as a component of garden soil.

Perennial
A plant whose life span extends over several growing seasons and that produces seeds in several growing seasons.

Petal
One of a series of flower parts lying within the sepals and next to the stamens and pistils, often large and brightly colored.

pH
A symbol for the hydrogen ion content of the soil, and thus a means of expressing the acidity or alkalinity of the soil.

Pistil
The female reproductive organ of a flower.

Pollen
Minute grains containing the male germ cells and released by the stamens.

Propagate
To produce new plants, either by vegetative means involving the rooting of pieces of a plant, or by sowing seeds.

Prostrate
Lying on the ground; creeping.

Rhizome
A horizontal underground stem, distinguished from a root by the presence of nodes and often enlarged by food storage.

Rootstock
The swollen, more or less elongate, underground stem of a perennial herb; a rhizome.

Rosette
A crowded cluster of leaves; usually basal, circular, and at ground level.

Runner
A prostrate shoot, rooting at its nodes.

Seed
A fertilized, ripened ovule, almost always covered with a protective coating and contained in a fruit.

Self-sow
To reproduce by dropping seeds.

Sepal
One of the outermost series of flower parts, arranged in a ring outside the petals, and usually green and leaflike.

Solitary
Borne singly or alone; not in clusters.

Species
A population of plants or animals whose members are at least potentially able to breed with each other, but which is reproductively isolated from other populations.

Spike
An elongated flower cluster whose individual flowers lack stalks.

Stamen
The male reproductive organ of a flower.

Subspecies
A naturally occurring geographical variant of a species.

Taproot
The main, central root of a plant.

Terminal
Borne at the tip of a stem or shoot, rather than in the axil.

Throat
The opening between the bases of the corolla lobes of a flower, leading into the corolla tube.

Toothed
Having the margin divided into small, toothlike segments.

Tuber
A swollen, mostly underground stem that bears buds and serves as a storage site for food.

Tufted
Growing in dense clumps, cushions, or tufts.

Two-lipped
Having two lips, as in certain irregular flowers.

Variegated
Marked, striped, or blotched with some color other than green.

Variety
A population of plants that differs consistently from the typical form of the species, either occurring naturally or produced in cultivation.

Vegetative propagation
Propagation by means other than seed.

Volunteer seedling
A plant that sprouts from seeds formed the previous year.

Whorl
A group of three or more leaves or shoots, all emerging from a stem at a single node.

PHOTO CREDITS

Sonja Bullaty and Angelo Lomeo ©, 43, 53

Thomas E. Eltzroth, 27, 28, 32, 35, 38, 40, 42, 70, 72, 76, 78, 83, 84, 86, 90, 91, 94, 98, 103

Entheos, 49

Derek Fell, 29, 50, 80

Judy Glattstein, 46, 95

Pamela J. Harper, 26, 33, 41, 44, 45, 56, 59, 60, 63, 64, 65, 68, 71, 75, 77, 81, 82, 87, 89, 92, 96, 100, 101, 102

Walter H. Hodge, 37, 51, 58, 85, 104

Peter Loewer, 54, 74

A. Peter Margosian, PHOTO/NATS ©, Cover

Gary Mottau, 31, 55

Ann Reilly, PHOTO/NATS ©, 2, 25

Joy Spurr, 66, 88

Steven M. Still, 30, 34, 36, 47, 48, 52, 57, 62, 67, 69, 73, 79, 93, 97, 99

Thomas K. Todsen, 39, 61

INDEX

CHANTICLEER PRESS
STEWART, TABORI & CHANG

Publisher
ANDREW STEWART

Senior Editor
ANN WHITMAN

Editor
CAROL McKEOWN

Project Editor
AMY HUGHES

Production
KATHY ROSENBLOOM
KARYN SLUTSKY

Design
JOSEPH RUTT